KNOTS, SPLICES AND FANCY WORK

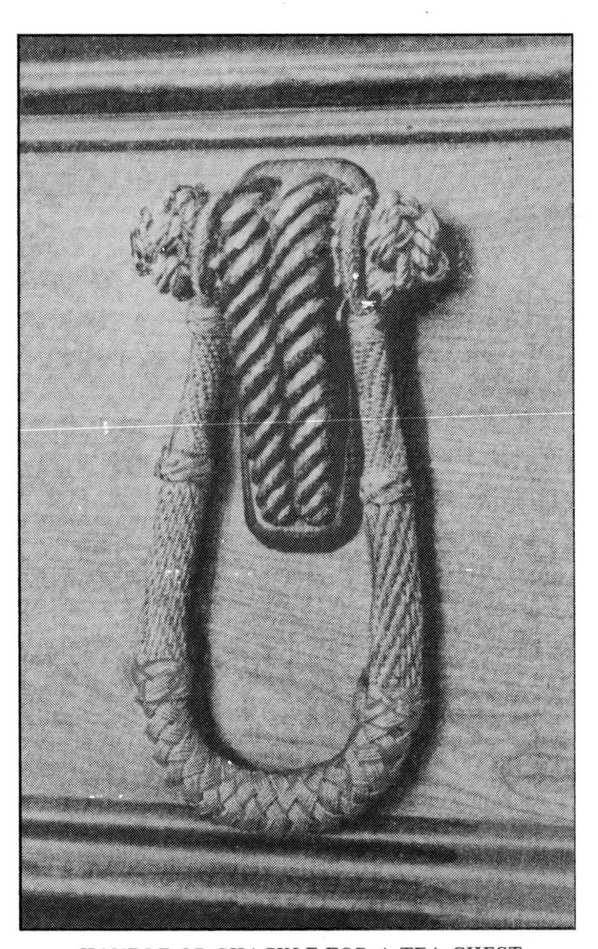

HANDLE OR SHACKLE FOR A TEA CHEST

SEA CHEST HANDLES. — The foundation of these is of four strand Rope. The strands were first tapered and then laid up again. Then at each end was worked a spindle or artificial eye. After being wormed the handle was tightly served all over. The centre part was then cross-pointed and then the spiral pointing was done with the ends of the cords used for cross-pointing and these were stoppered down. The next parts were then covered with palm and needle hitching and then the eyes were covered with cockscombing. Long Footrope Knots were then worked over the ends of the different patterns.

To make the cross piece, six strands of suitably sized stuff were laid up round a core of metal bar and a Star Knot, crowned, worked on one end. Then the cross piece was passed through the eyes of the handle and a Star Knot, crowned, was worked on the other end.

[*Frontispiece.*

KNOTS, SPLICES
AND FANCY WORK

BY

CHAS. L. SPENCER
(Revised by P. W. BLANDFORD)

GLASGOW
BROWN, SON & FERGUSON, LTD., NAUTICAL PUBLISHERS
4-10 DARNLEY STREET

First Edition	-	1934
Fifth Edition	-	1956
Reprinted	-	1958
Revised	-	1964
Reprinted	-	1969
Reprinted	-	1974
Reprinted	-	1978
Reprinted	-	1992
Reprinted	-	1997

ISBN 0 85174 157 6

Printed and Made in Great Britain

PREFACE

(TO THE FIRST FOUR EDITIONS)

FROM time immemorial men seem to have been interested in Fancy Knots. An early recorded instance is the Gordian Knot that was cut by Alexander the Great — but he was a "sodger"! In later times we have the wonderful interlaced ornaments of Celtic work.

The art of Fancy Knotting as practised at sea probably reached its height on board the sperm whalers about the middle of the XIXth Century. Some of the chest handles or shackles of that period are perfect examples of design and of craftsmanship.

Since the advent of steam the art has declined. There are very few of the old-time shellbacks alive now, and there is a danger that much of the Fancy Work may be lost altogether. This book is an effort to preserve it.

No doubt some Knots and Fancy Work used at sea are not here recorded and it is to be hoped that anyone knowing them will publish that knowledge.

Even on yachts it is rare that any fancy work is to be seen except perhaps on the manropes and, occasionally, on the yoke lines, and these are generally supplied by the riggers or the sailmakers. Something better than that might be expected and probably would be produced if owners and crew realised the possibilities. Of late years a false standard of smartness seems to have been set up. It consists in scrubbing decks and polishing brasswork. These are all very well but are jobs that can be done by anyone. Good rope work is a sailor's job.

The whole of Captain Jutsum's book *Knots and Splices*, has been incorporated in this volume and, as far as possible, only Seagoing Knots are shewn. The aim of the book is to describe Fancy Work and such of the Ordinary Knots as are used in making it.

There are, of course, Knots that come under both headings of Fancy and Ordinary. I included the Spritsail Sheet Knot, for instance. It may be called Fancy because I doubt if anyone alive has seen it used as a Spritsail Sheet Knot — the spritsail in question being the squaresail set under the bowsprit.

By the way, who and what was Matthew Walker? The query has often been put but I have seen no answer. He is the only man after whom a Knot, known under the same name for generations, has been called.

As to the making of Knots themselves, it should be kept in mind by beginners that all Knots and Fancy Work are made up of a very few simple turns and tucks. I think they could be counted on the fingers. The skill to be attained is that required by a man in handling several strands at once and in recognising where to make the tuck. The art consists in making the combinations of the simple elements. Incidentally, it may be remarked that the finished works looks far better than any illustration!

As already stated, Captain Jutsum's work has been taken as a basis. The additions come from many sources. The Wire Grommet has been included as the making of one is usually a mystery; I am indebted to Captain Stopford, R.N., for permission to reproduce the description from his *Cordage and Cables*. The Star Knot was described for the first time in the *Yachting Monthly*. From the same source came very good descriptions of some other, better known, Knots and, by courtesy of the Editor, the tail piece.

So far as I know, the Square Plait or Square Sennit of one part has never before been described in a book. I got it from Quartermaster Higgins of the "City Line". I am also indebted to Lieut. Commdr. W. Haynes, Jesmond, Newcastle-on-Tyne, for instructions regarding making "Square Sennit of 12 or of 16 Strands".

Some of the Mats and Ocean Plaits were described in the *Nautical Magazine*, and other items have been picked up or evolved over a period of years.

I have to thank Mr. Archie MacMillan, Fairlie, for his Perfect Wire Grommet; Mr. Ian A. D. Wilson for the Long Turk's Head; Mr. R. D. Younson for the Russian Mat, and Capt. E. W. Denison, R.N., for much assistance.

I have the greatest pleasure in thanking Captain E. W. Denison, R.N.; Messrs. R. D. Younson, J. L. Aldridge, F. S. Martin, A. Greenstock, F. W. E. Bedwell, Geo. Bruce, and H. H. Gillman for their help and for the trouble, they have taken.

Especially I have to thank 1st Lieut. Antonio M. Esparteiro of the Portuguese Navy, for sending me many very beautiful and interesting knots the description of which, I believe, has never before been given in English.

My thanks for several items are due to Mr. John Alexander, especially for his very ingenious method of making Turk's Head knots by means of a "former", Mr. Roy Melcome for his Double Carrick Single Sennit, and Mr. Clifford W. Ashley for permission to include a knot and two patterns of Herringbone Weave, and to Mr. Hugh Sisam for a variant of the Studding Sail Halliard Hitch.

I would like to make an attempt to disarm criticisms on the nomenclature of knots. I have found many instances of different names for the same knot and of different knots bearing the same name and I have had to compromise in some cases.

It is recognised that the book cannot be a complete and final collection of Fancy Work (for instance, I have no knowledge of the drawn thread and tassel work that was done on sea chest covers), but I believe it to be a more complete collection than anything yet published.

CHAS. L. SPENCER.

PREFACE TO THE FIFTH EDITION

As the late Chas. L. Spencer says, this book can never be a complete and final collection of knots, but as the need for another edition has become evident, an opportunity has been taken to add to it yet again. Many new knots have been added and I have redrawn some illustrations to improve their clarity. Lashings have been included for the first time, and the small but important whippings have been brought into line with modern practice.

Much of my own knotting knowledge came from the first edition of this book. I hope that readers will find that this edition makes an even greater contribution to the art of knotting and that, within the bounds set by the need for keeping to an economic price, this is still a more complete collection than anything yet published.

PERCY W. BLANDFORD.

CONTENTS

Knots, Splices and Fancy Work

THE CONSTRUCTION OF ROPES.

ROPE, the term being used in its widest construction, is made from almost every pliable material, but is generally composed of hemp, manila, coir, cotton, sisal, steel, iron or copper wire, and more recently nylon and other plastics.

For the present we will confine ourselves to those having their origin in the vegetable kingdom, and more especially to those made from hemp and manila.

These are divided into three classes:—

1. A **Hawser-laid Rope,** which is composed of three strands laid up generally right-handed (that is, the direction taken by the strands in forming the rope runs always from left to right) (Fig. 1).
2. A **Shroud-laid Rope,** also laid up right-handed, but consisting of four strands (Fig. 2) with a heart in the centre.

Fig. 1. Fig. 2.

3. **A Cable-laid Rope,** which is composed of three right-handed hawser-laid ropes laid up together left-handed, so that it may be said to consist of nine strands (Fig. 3).

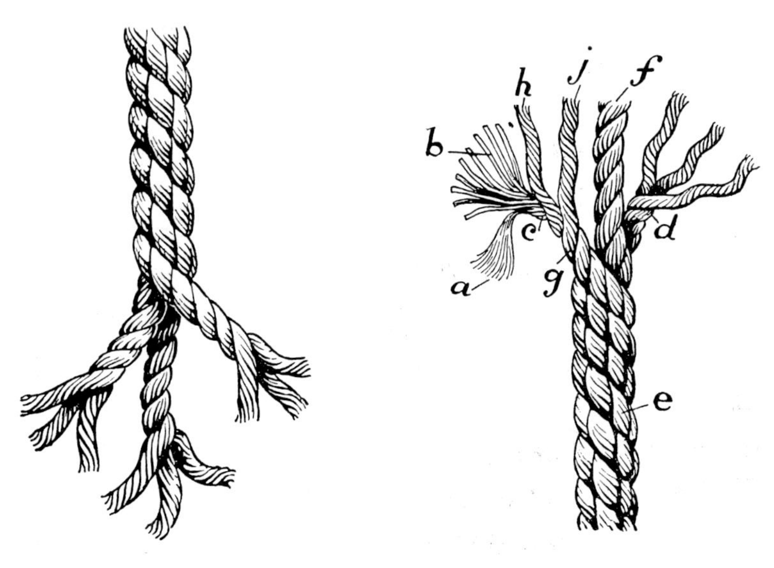

Fig. 3. Fig. 4.

In Fig. 4 we show a more complete analysis of its construction.

First we see the cable *e* formed by the three ropes *d, f,* and *g*; whilst the rope *g* is dissected to show the strands forming it, *c, h, j*; and in the strand *c* we see *b*, the yarn composing the strand, and *a* a yarn teased out to show the original fibre.

The following are the kinds of rope generally in use.

Hemp.—A strong, rather rough rope. Used more than any other on shipboard.

Coir.—Made from the fibre of coconut husks. It is light, will float on water, very elastic, very rough, about ¼ strength of hemp.

Manila.—Made from the fibre of plantain leaves. It is strong, of fine appearance, smooth, runs well over blocks, is generally used on yachts.

Sisal.—Made from the fibre of aloe leaves. Very white, about as strong as hemp and stands sea water well. Rope of sisal is now issued to the Royal Navy.

Cotton.—Very smooth, white, will stand much running over blocks. Used for machinery driving ropes, not so strong as hemp or manila. Used for manropes, etc., on yachts.

Italian Hemp.—The strongest rope. Very smooth, very nice to handle and to work. Does not become hard when wet, runs well over blocks. Lightly tarred, it is the best rope for running rigging. Used white for sheets. Dearer than manila but lasts longer, say four or five seasons on a yacht as against two or three seasons with manila.

Nylon.—Synthetic, smooth, water resistant, elastic. Attractive for fancy work.

Six Strand Rope.—Six strand rope of many sizes is made and used in France where it is called "Septin" (six strands and the heart making seven).

It is very smooth but not so strong as three strand.

It is useful for some fancy knots such as the Star Knot.

Braided Ropes.—Braided ropes are used for log lines, signal halliards, etc. They are really round sennit and are usually of eight strands worked round a heart.

These strands consist of yarns laid parallel, that is to say not twisted, so that when the rope is unlaid the strands are loose. Braided rope is difficult to splice but is easy to form an artificial or spindle eye on it.

By unlaying the rope and then laying up the yarns into nettles and these into strands, fancy knots can be made. Splices can be made with braided ropes though the process is laborious. As a rule, the rope is braided so tightly that there is no room to tuck the strands. The first thing to do, therefore, is to "unbraid" the rope sufficiently far down, put on a whipping and braid it up again as described under "Round Sennit", but not too tightly.

If an eye splice is required, form an artificial or spindle eye and tuck the strands down the slackened part of the rope following the strands.

If a short splice is required, marry the strands and tuck.

Whipping.—The end of a rope must be secured in some way to prevent the strands fraying out. This is usually done by whipping—binding with twine or stout thread, preferably waxed. A common whipping is made by laying the line along the rope and wrapping over it towards the end (Fig. 5A), preferably against the lay. When nearly enough turns have been made, turn back the short end (Fig. 5B), then make three more turns and pass the working end through the loop (Fig. 5C). Pull back on the short end, so as to bury the working end, and cut off the surplus (Fig. 5D).

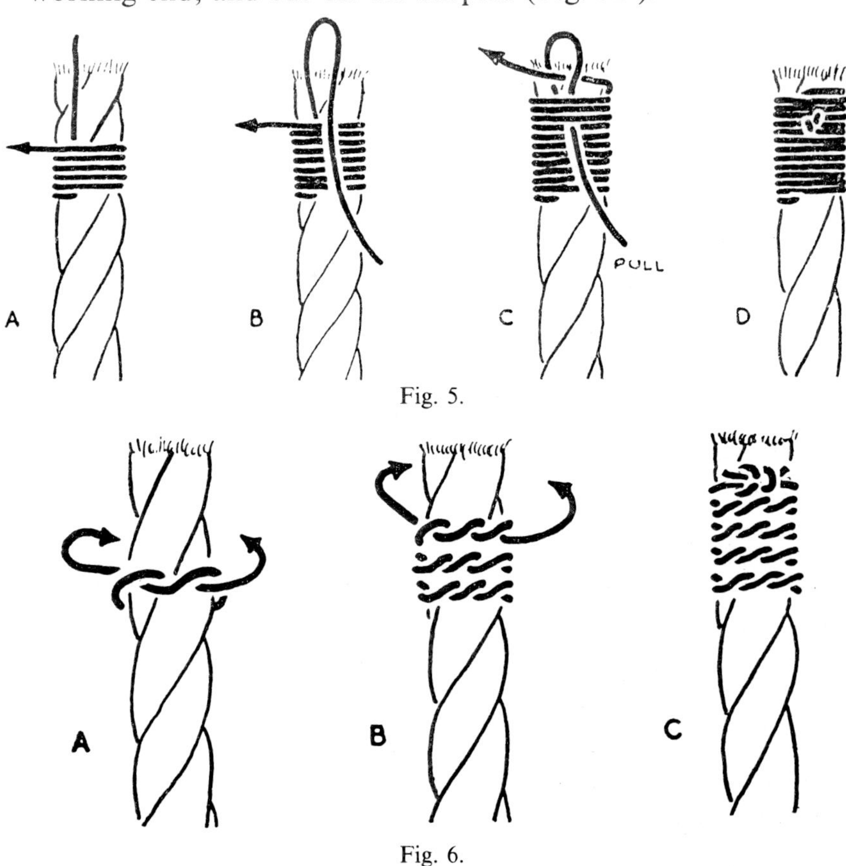

Fig. 5.

Fig. 6.

An alternative is a West Country whipping (Fig. 6). Put the middle of the line behind the rope and knot in front (Fig. 6A). Make another knot behind, and continue knotting in front and behind along the rope (Fig. 6B). When sufficient turns have been made, finish with a reef knot (Fig. 6C).

The most secure whipping has the line passing through the rope. This may be done with a needle, but the sailmaker's whipping (Fig. 7) gets the same result without a needle. Open the strands and lay the line in, with a loop loosely encircling one strand, and a long and a short end projecting from the opposite space (Fig. 7A). Lay up the strands again, hold the loop and the short end along the rope, and put on the whipping turns (Fig. 7B). Lift the loop and place it around the strand it is already encircling, then pull the short end (Fig. 7C). Let the short end follow up the outside of the space it is projecting from and tie it to the long end in the centre of the end of the rope (Fig. 7D).

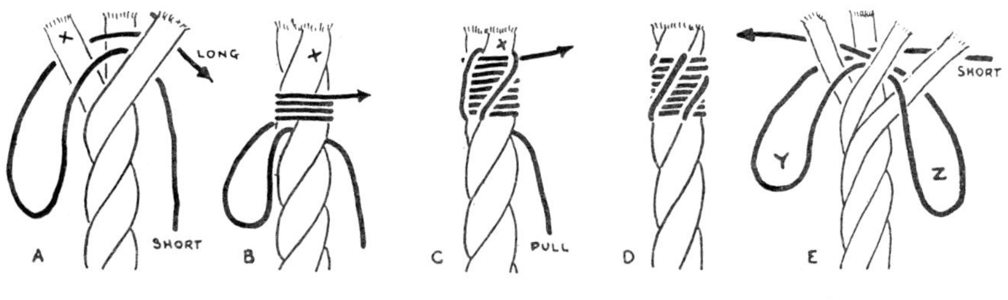

Fig. 7.

With four-strand rope a sailmaker's whipping must be started with two loops (Fig. 7E). After putting on the turns, take loop *Z* over the end of its strand and pull loop *Y* to tighten it. Put loop Y over its strand and pull the short end to tighten it. Take the short end up and tie it to the long end.

For extra security and decoration a plain whipping on a large rope may be finished by snaking (Fig. 8). The line is taken through the rope with a needle, then it is looped in turn over the end turns to form a pattern, and finally taken through the rope again to finish off.

Fig. 8.

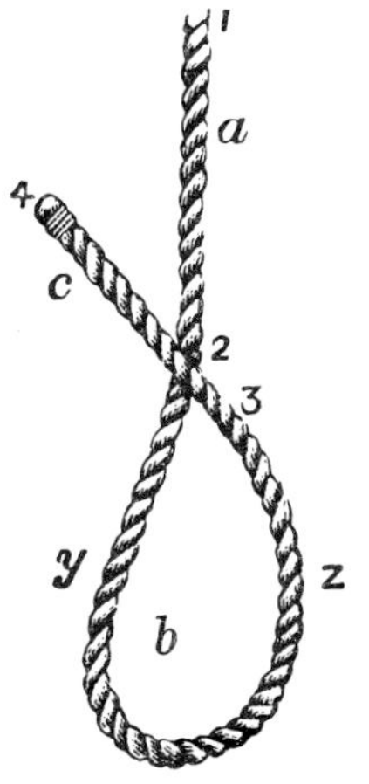

Fig. 9.

Fig. 9 shows a common loop, by which most of the following knots, etc., are commenced. Note exactly how the loop lies, and let us letter its parts clearly for future reference. The part of rope extending from 1 to 2 is known as the standing part which we will call *a*, the portion included between 2 and 3 following round the loop by *y* and *z* is termed the bight which we will call *b*, and from 3 to 4 is known as the end *c*.

Then starting in each case from the position shown in Fig. 8 we make the following knots, etc.:—

An Overhand Knot.—Place *c* up through bight *b*, and draw taut (Fig. 10).

A Figure of Eight Knot.—Back *c* round behind *a*, bring over part *z* and dip down through bight *b* and haul taut (Fig. 11).

Fig. 11.

Fig. 10.

A Multiple Overhand Knot.—If the twist of a simple overhand knot are carried round two or three times, a more bulky stopper knot is formed (Fig. 12).

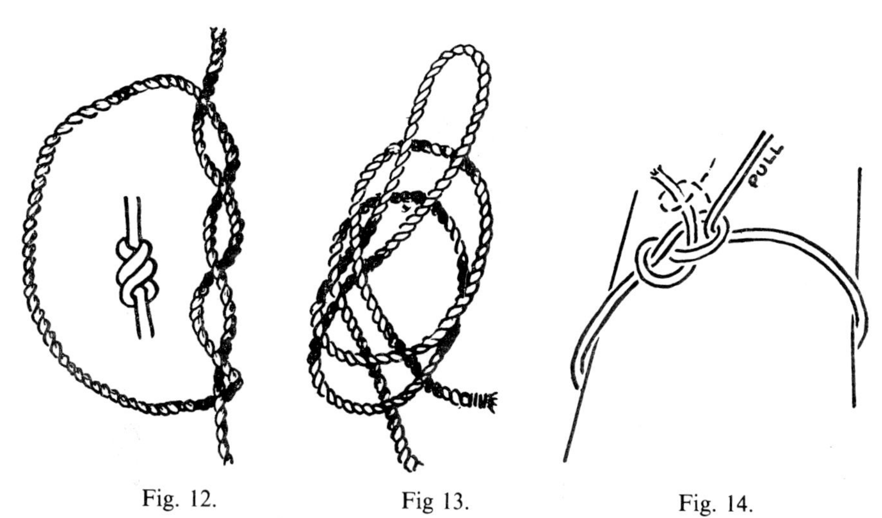

Fig. 12. Fig 13. Fig. 14.

A Double Overhand Knot.—If the end of the rope is looped before tying the knot, a larger stopper knot is formed

(Fig. 13), or the knot may be used to form an eye, but this is not as satisfactory as a bowline.

A Packer's Knot.—A Figure of Eight knot is made around the standing part to tighten the line around a parcel, then the knot is secured by putting a half-hitch around the end, as shown dotted (Fig. 14).

A Bowline.—Reverting to our original loop (Fig. 9), first taking part *z* in the right hand with *y* in the left, throw a loop over *c*, the end, as in Fig. 15.

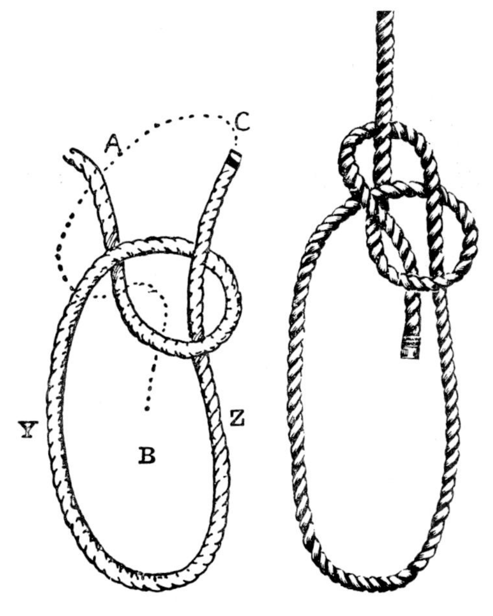

Fig. 15. Fig. 16.

Secondly, lead *c* round behind part *a* and pass it down through the last made loop, as indicated by the dotted line, and haul taut as in Fig. 16.

A Running Bowline.—Form a loop with a long end *c* lying underneath the standing part *a* (Fig. 17).

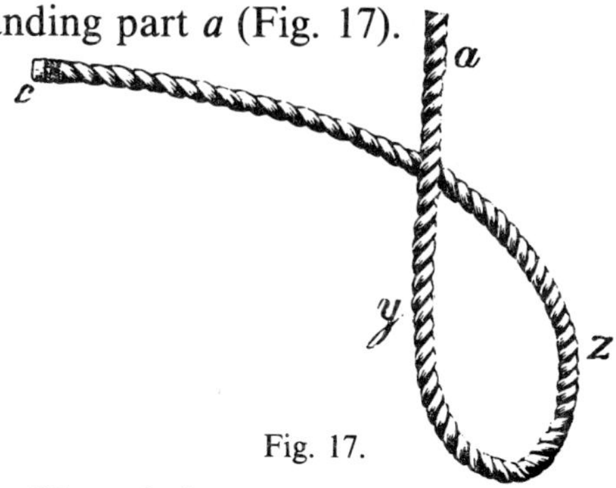

Fig. 17.

Fig. 18.

Now bring end *c* over part *y* and with it form the bowline knot on part *z* just as in the previous case we formed it on its own part, when it will appear as in Fig. 18. It is used whenever a running noose is required.

French Bowline.—This is begun in the same way as the simple Bowline, but instead of passing *C* (Fig. 15, page 9) round behind *A, C* is taken round again parallel to *Y* and passed through the loop. It is then taken behind *A* and down through the loop in the same way as for the simple Bowline.

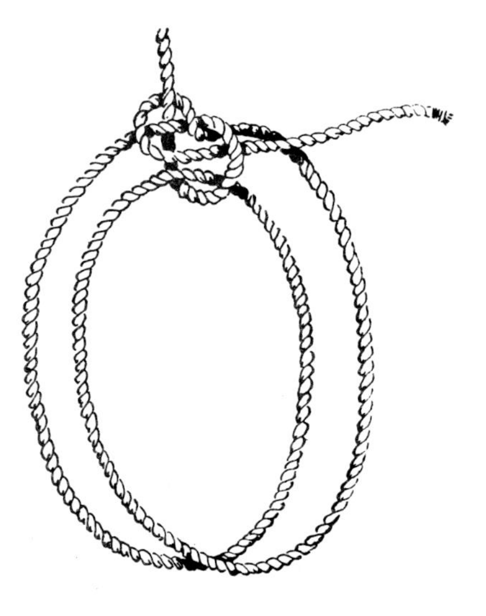

Fig. 19.

This is a useful knot for slinging an insensible man. He is put sitting on one bight and the other is passed under his armpits and across his back. His weight keeps this tight and he cannot fall out.

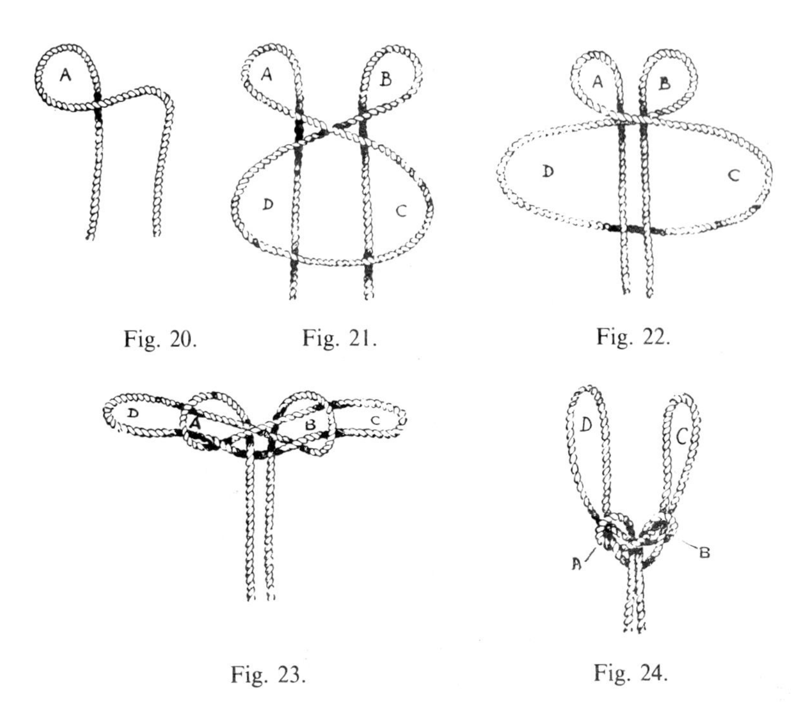

Fig. 20. Fig. 21. Fig. 22.

Fig. 23. Fig. 24.

Spanish Bowline.—This is a Bowline with two bights. Begin as shewn in Fig. 20. Then as in Fig. 21. The large bight *DC* is now dipped over to the back of *A* and *B* as shewn in Fig. 22. Bight *D* is then put through bight *A* and bight *C* is put through bight *B* as shewn in Fig. 23 and worked tight as shewn in Fig. 24.

The formation of a Half Hitch (Fig. 25) and two half hitches (Fig. 26) is sufficiently indicated by those diagrams.

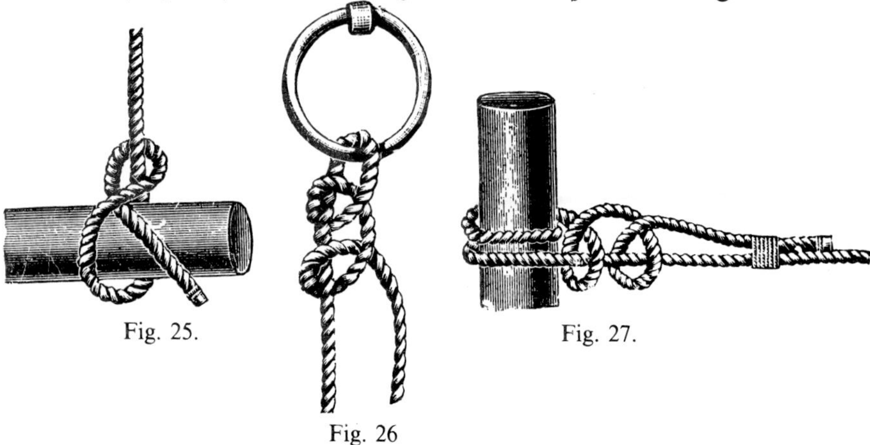

Fig. 25.

Fig. 27.

Fig. 26

The commonest method of making a rope's end fast to a bollard, etc., is by taking a round turn and two half hitches and stopping the end back for further security (Fig. 27).

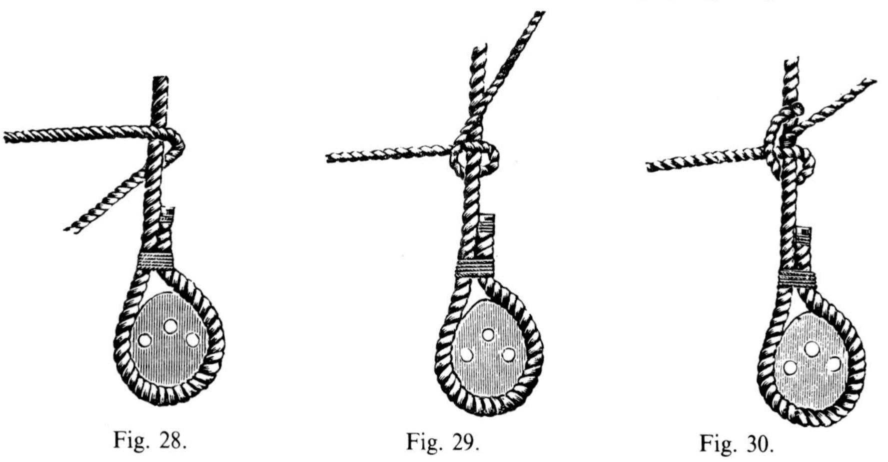

Fig. 28.

Fig. 29.

Fig. 30.

A Clove Hitch is really a jamming form of two half hitches, and is principally used when a small rope has to be secured to a larger one and the end still kept free to pass along for further purposes, as in securing ratlines to the shrouds. Its formation is shown in three successive stages (Figs. 28, 29, 30).

Stopper Hitch or Rolling Hitch.—This is a hitch used for securing the tail of a handy billy to a rope, or when hanging off a rope with a stopper.

Take a half hitch, against the lay, with the tail round the rope as shewn in Fig. 31.

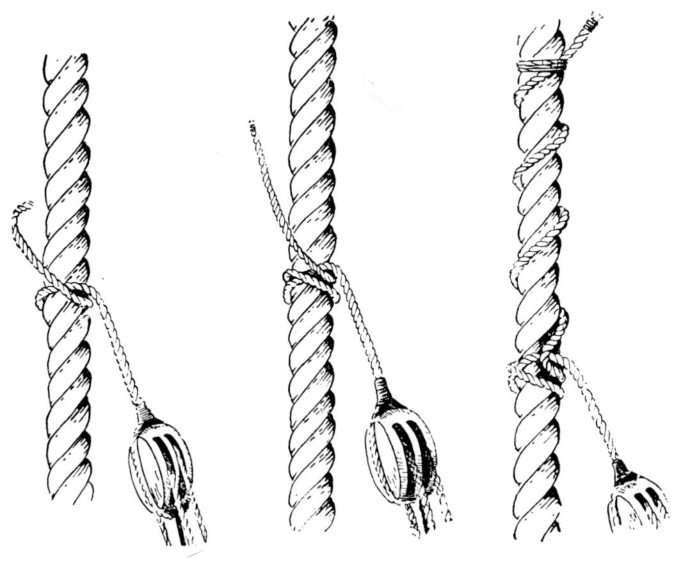

Fig. 31. Fig. 32. Fig. 33.

Then take the tail round the rope again, under the standing part of the tail and riding on the first hitch, as shewn in Fig. 32. Then complete as shewn in Fig. 33 or tuck the end under itself as in finishing a clove hitch.

A Timber Hitch is a useful way of securing a rope quickly to a plank, but when there is to be a long and continuous strain, or when it is required to keep the end of a piece of timber pointed steadily in one direction, it should be supplemented with a half hitch (Figs. 34 and 35).

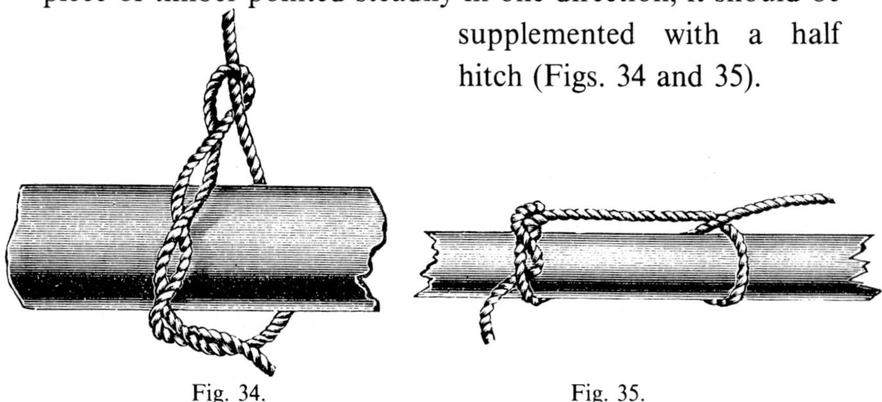

Fig. 34. Fig. 35.

The timber hitch itself consists simply of a half hitch taken with a rather long end, which is used up by twisting it back around its own part of the hitch. In Fig. 34 the hitch is purposely left very loose so that its information may be the more easily seen.

A Fisherman's Bend is formed by taking two round turns around the object to which the rope is to be secured, and then backing the end round in the form of a half hitch under both the standing part and second round turn. The end may be further secured by taking a half hitch around its own part or by stopping it to it (Figs. 36, 37), the dotted line showing the next direction the end *c* must take.

It is used when securing a hauling line to the ring of the kedge, or for bending a rope to a bucket, etc., and is often called a bucket hitch.

Fig. 36.

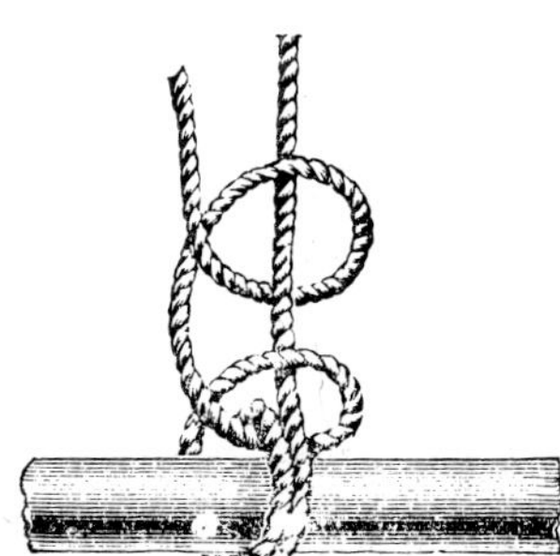

Fig. 37.

A Topsail Halyard Bend.—This bend is never seen in deep water ships, but is sometimes used on board yachts. It is commenced in a similar manner to a fisherman's bend, but three round turns are first taken around the spar, the end

Fig. 38.

Fig. 39.

being backed around the standing part *a* and then led under all three turns as in Fig. 38, and then again backed over the last two round turns and under the first, as shown in Fig. 39.

A Stunsail Halyard Bend is simply a "Fisherman's Bend" with the end backed again over the last round turn and under the first (Fig. 40).

Fig. 40.

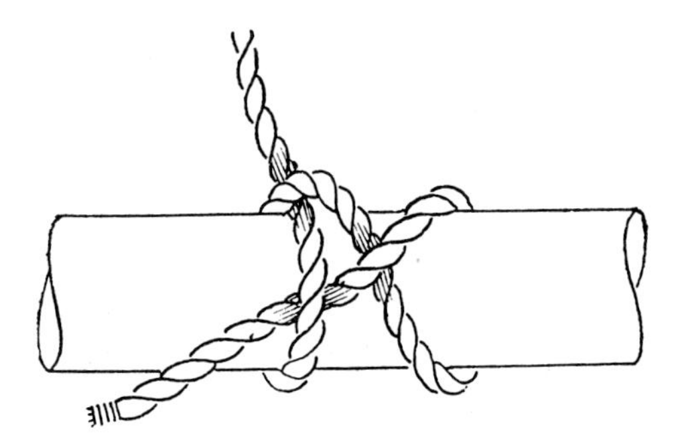

Fig. 41.

Stunsail Halyard Bend. This is another way. It will not slip either way and will not work loose. (Also called Ground Line Hitch).

A Blackwall Hitch is a quick way of temporarily securing a rope to a hook. As will be seen from the illustration (Fig. 42), it consists of a half hitch, the standing part *a* as soon as it receives the strain jamming the end part *c*. It holds much more firmly than would be imagined at first sight. By taking another round turn at *b*, before passing the end *c* under *a*, it will hold more securely.

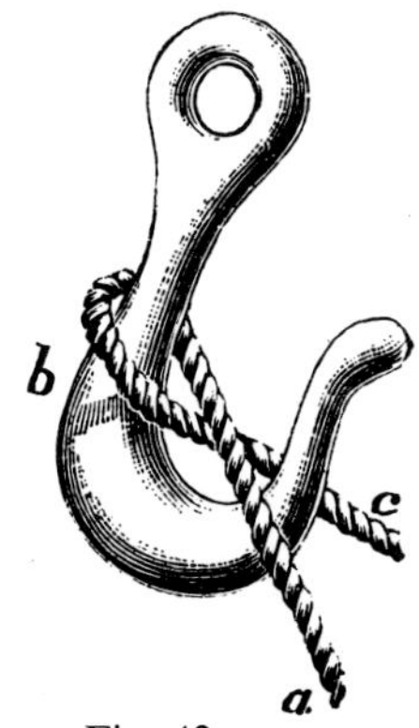

Fig. 42.

A Midshipman's Hitch is sometimes used instead of a "Blackwall Hitch", and will hold better if the rope is at all greasy. It is made by first forming a "Blackwall Hitch" and then taking the underneath part and placing it over the bill of the hook (Fig. 43).

A Double Blackwall Hitch is made by taking the bight of the rope and placing it across the neck of the strop of the block, crossing it behind, then placing the under part over the hook and crossing the upper part on top of it (Fig. 44). It holds better than either of the two preceding hitches.

Fig. 43.

Fig. 44.

Shamrock Knot.—Make an overhand knot as at *a* (Fig. 45), bring the end round and up through the bight at *b* and make another overhand knot as at *c*. Push bight *d* through the middle of knot *a*, and *e* through knot *c*. Pull all taut and the result is as Fig. 46.

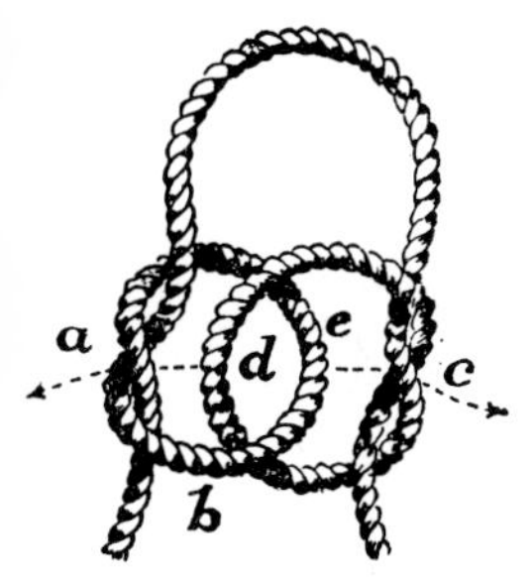

Fig. 45.

Fig. 46.

Triangle Knot.—Also called "Sacred, or Brahmin Knot". This knot can be made on an endless rope "circle". It is reputed to be in use ceremonially by Brahmins.

Commence by laying a bight back over the two parts *AA* as in Fig. 47.

Keeping the bight in position, lay the two parts *AA* up over it, the loops *CC* being hitched round the little finger (Fig. 48).

Untwist and lay one of the bights *B*1 over the parts *AA* and the bight *B*2 as in Fig. 49.

Fig. 47.

Fig. 48.

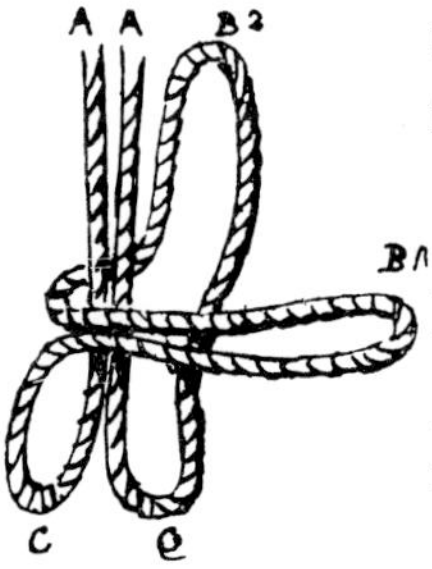

Fig. 49.

Untwist and lay the other bight *B*2 over *B*1 and through the loops *CC* in Fig. 50 and work tight.

The front of the finished knot is shewn in Fig. 51 and the back in Fig. 52.

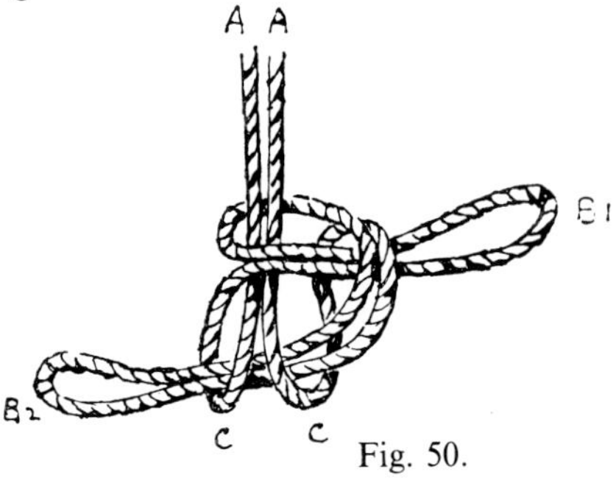

Fig. 50.

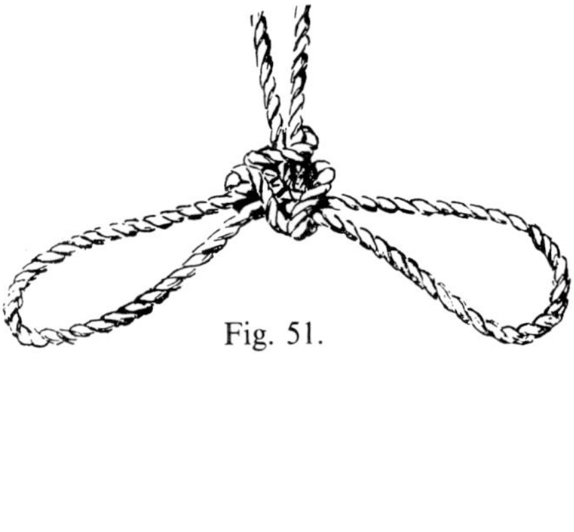

Fig. 51.

Fig. 52.

Square Knot.—Make a loop with *DA* round *CB* (Fig. 53). Bring *B* up behind loop *DA*, over and down in front of *DA*, keeping a sufficient opening where *B* passes up and behind *A* by inserting a finger (Fig. 54).

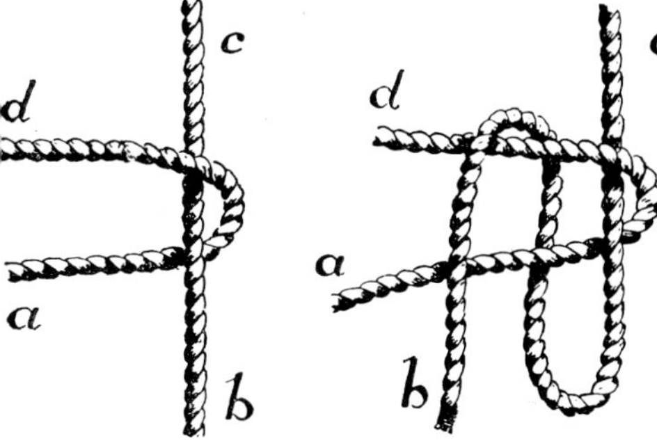

Fig. 53. Fig. 54.

Bring end *A* in front of end *B* and end *A* through loop in *CB* as shown in Fig. 55.

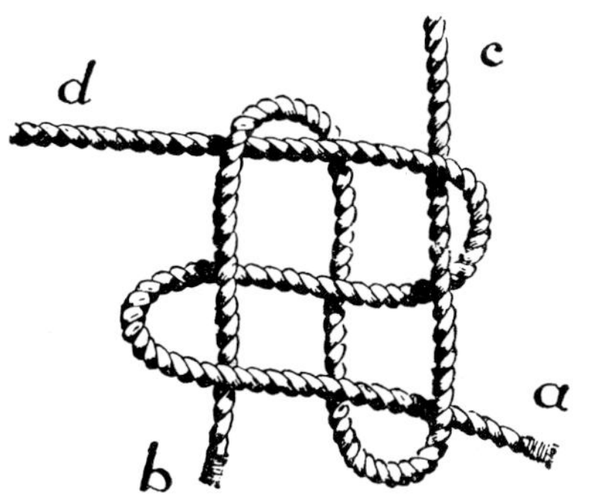

Fig. 55.

Tighten up ends equally and the result will be as in Fig. 56, front, and 57, back

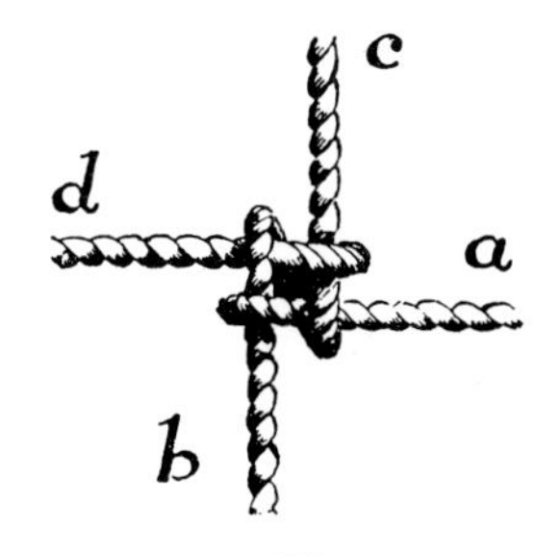

Fig. 56.

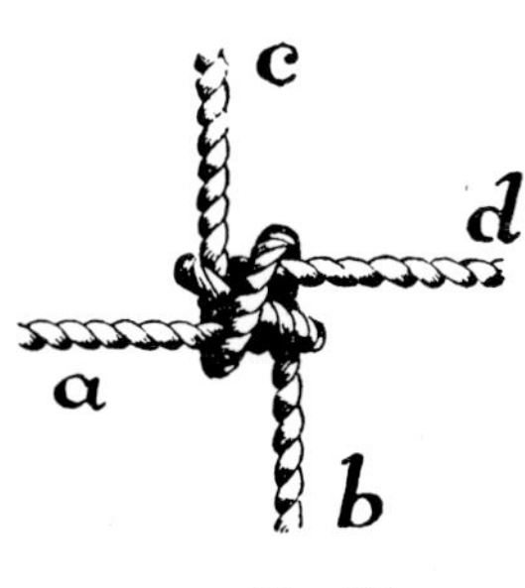

Fig. 57.

A Monkey's Fist.—This knot was often worked on to the end of a heaving line to give it weight and make it "carry".

Make a hank of, say, three turns, then take three turns round the waist of the hank with the working end *W*. Then lead the working end through the loops of the original hank and over the three turns that were put round the waist. Do this three times (Fig. 58).

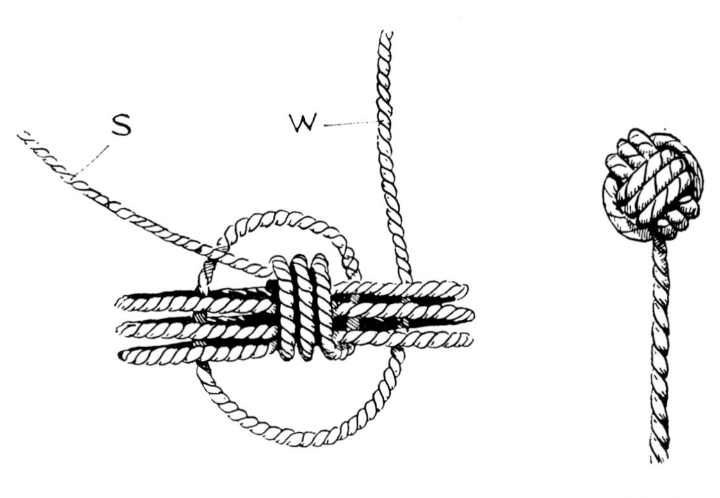

Fig. 58.

Fig. 59.

Work the knot tight and cut off the working end, or splice it into the standing part (Fig. 59).

On the figures the standing end is marked *S* and the working end *W*.

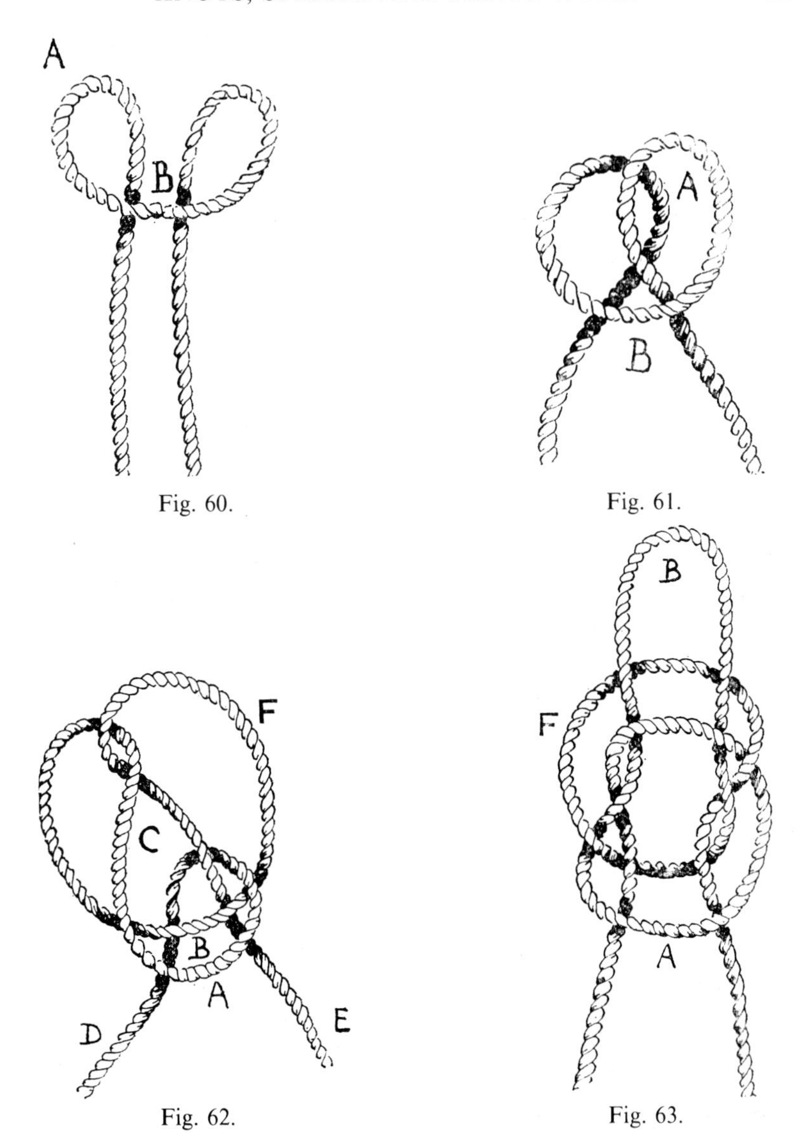

Fig. 60.

Fig. 61.

Fig. 62.

Fig. 63.

Bag Knot, Bottle Knot, or Beggarman's Knot.—This knot is used to close the end of a bag and form a handle by which it may be carried. It is also used to make a handle or sling with which to carry a bottle or jar. It is then worked round the flange of the neck. The two ends of the line may be knotted or spliced together, thus making two carrying loops. The knot is also known as the "Beggarman's Knot" by fishermen, who use it for fastening bladder floats to their nets.

Begin as in Fig. 60. Then cross one loop over the other as in Fig. 61. Then take the loop at *A* and turn it back beyond *B*, holding them both in position, as shewn in Fig. 62. Then put thumb and forefinger down through the opening *C*, under the standing part *D*, catch *B* and pull it up through *C*, keeping hold of *D* and *E*, and allowing the loop at *F* to dip down behind the knot (Fig. 63).

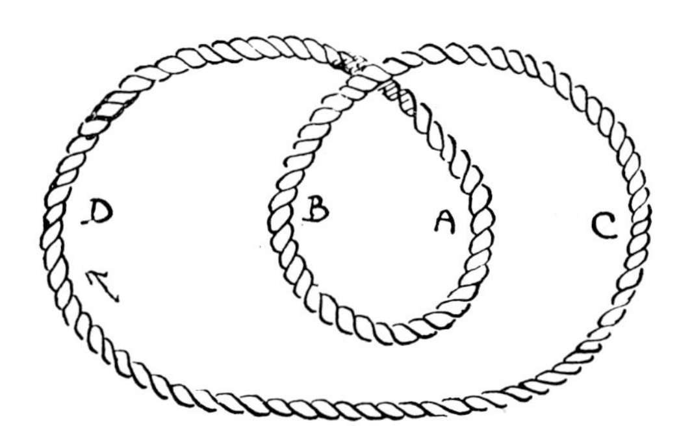

Fig. 64.—Single Bottle Knot.

Single Bottle Knot.—This is used for slinging an object with a rim or flange. It is not so secure as the Bottle or Bag Knot.

It is made by knotting or splicing the ends of the cord so as to form a sling and then making a bight on it, as shewn in Fig. 64. Then take part *A* to the right and over *C* and part *B* to the left and under *D* as shewn in Fig. 65.

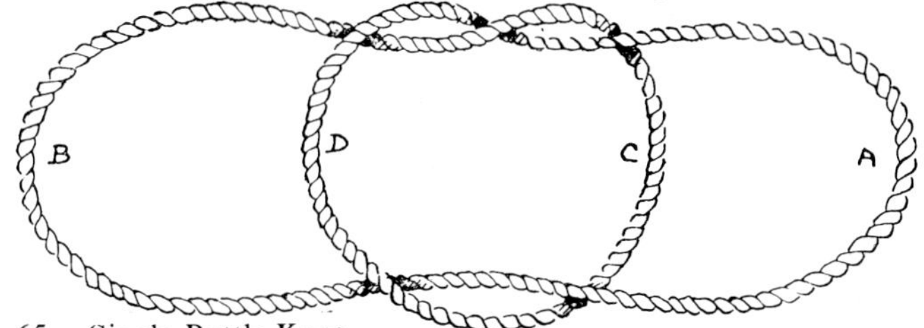

Fig. 65.—Single Bottle Knot.

The centre loop is slipped over the object and hauled taut. The side loops may be used as handles.

The Marline Hitch (Fig. 66) is used to bend sails to spars, make up hammocks, etc.

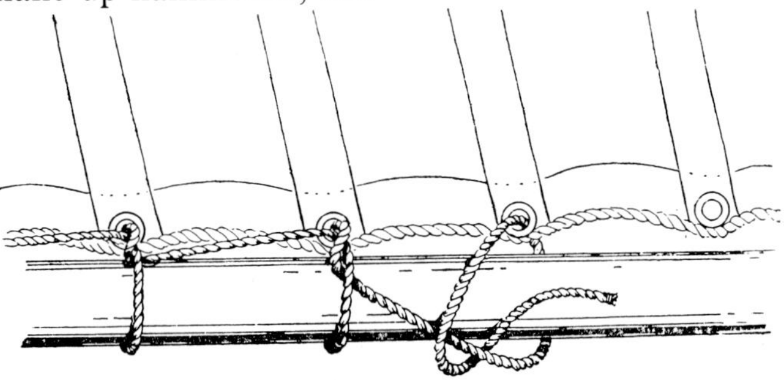

Fig. 66.

The line is carried round the back of the spar, through the eyelet, then with an overhead hitch, and hauled tight.

KNOTS, Etc., MADE ON THE BIGHT OF A ROPE, THAT IS, WITHOUT UTILISING THE ENDS.

A Bowline on the Bight.—Using both parts of the rope together, commence as in making an ordinary bowline (Fig.67). To finish off, open out bight *c*, and taking it in the direction indicated by the dotted line, pass the whole knot through it and haul taut, when it will appear as in Fig 68.

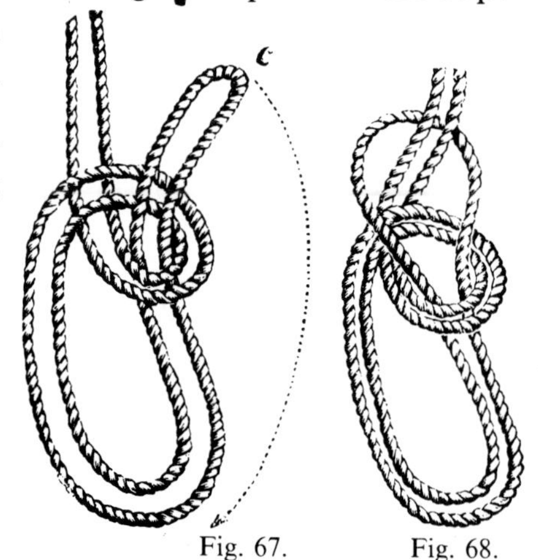

Fig. 67. Fig. 68.

A Marline-Spike Hitch is used for getting a purchase with a marline-spike, capstan bar, etc., when putting on a seizing or lashing. By Fig. 69 it will be seen to consist of the standing part picked through a loop laid over it, so that the spike lies under the standing part and over the sides of the loop.

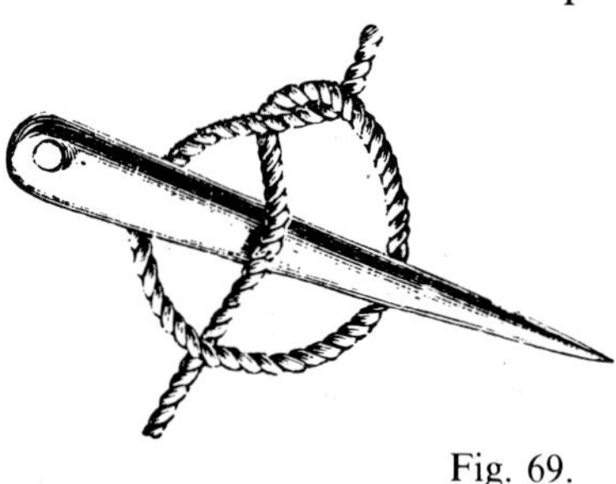
Fig. 69.

Draw Hitch.—This is used for fastening a rope to a post, ring, etc., when instantaneous release is desired. It will stand a strain but a sharp pull on the running end *R* casts the whole thing adrift.

Begin as in Fig. 70 with the bight *A* of the rope round the back of the bar. Then make another bight *B* with the standing end *S* and pass it through the bight *A* as shewn in Fig. 71 and pull end *R* tight.

Then make a third bight *C* with the running end *R* and pass it through the bight *B*, and pull part *S* tight. This effectually locks the hitch (Fig. 72).

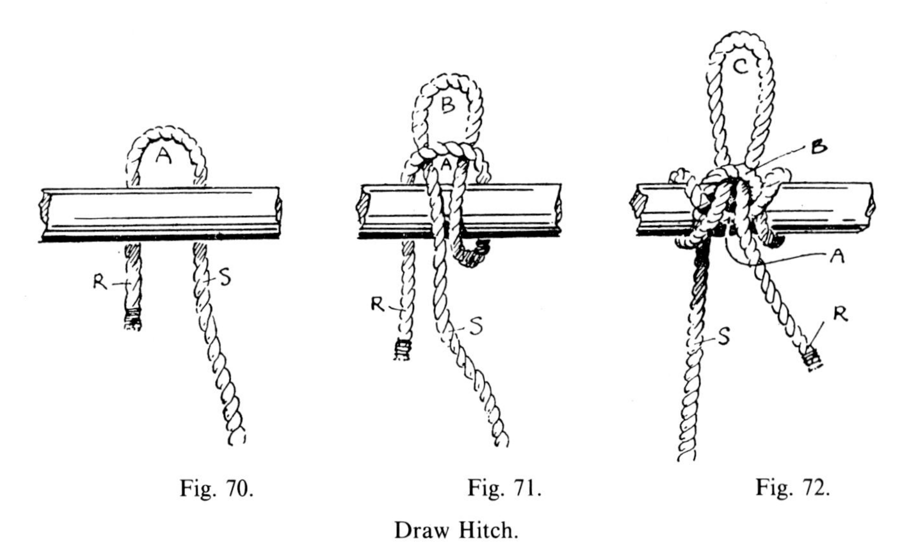

Fig. 70. Fig. 71. Fig. 72.

Draw Hitch.

Ossel Knot and Ossel Hitch. The heavy roping round a net is called the backing and the rope along the top of the net is called the headrope. These are connected by short pieces called "Ossels".

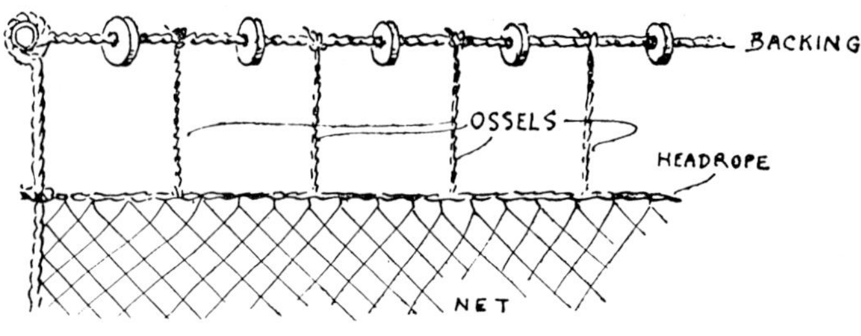

Fig. 73.

Ossel Knot.—With the working part *A* make a turn to the left riding over part *B*, and with the thumb of the left hand inserted under the turn at *C*. Make a second turn also riding over *B*. Make a third turn with *A* bringing it to the right of *B* and carry the end across the three turns and under

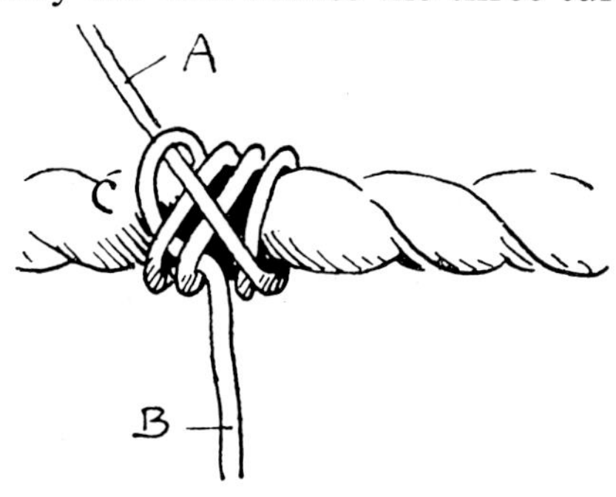

OSSEL KNOT.

Fig. 74.

at *C*. Haul taut. This is a useful knot that will not slip or come adrift.

Ossel Hitch.—Take the working part *A* down behind the headrope *C* and bring it up in front of *C* and left of *B*. Take it round behind *B*, down in front of *C*, round behind *C*, over its own part and *B* and out under at *E*.

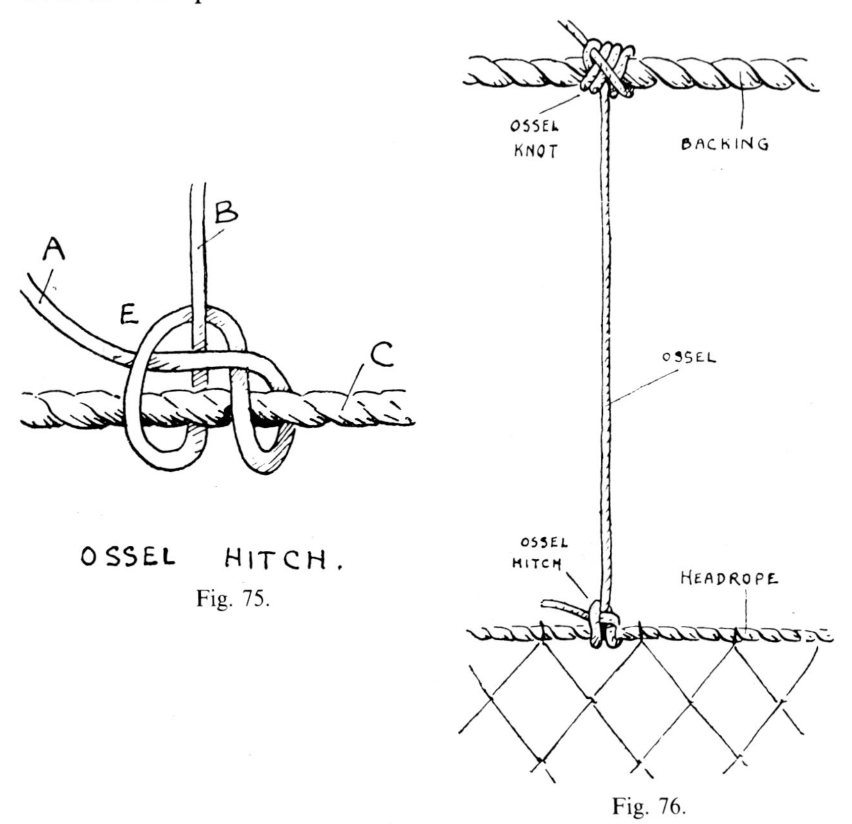

Fig. 75.

Fig. 76.

Magnus Hitch.—This hitch is used by builders on scaffolding work. It will not slip along a pole. It is really a Clove Hitch with an extra turn.

With the working end *A* take two turns to the right of the standing part *B*. Carry the working end *A* over to the left and take another turn bringing the end through the bight and to the left of the standing part *B* (Fig. 77).

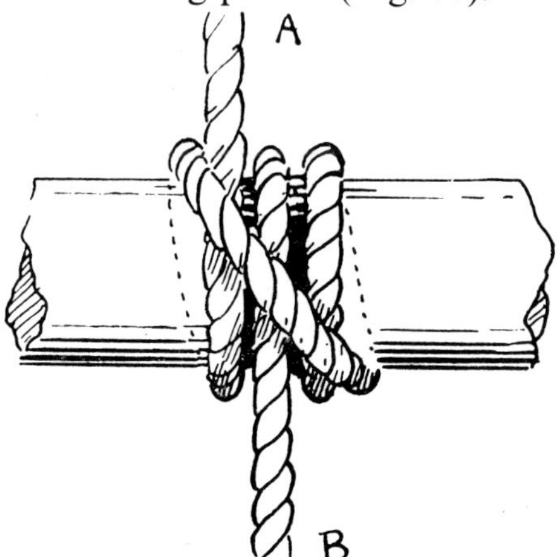

Fig. 77.—Magnus Hitch.

A Sheepshank is used for shortening a rope. Gather up the amount desired in the form of Fig. 78.

Fig. 78.

Then with parts *a* and *b* form a half hitch round the two parts of the bight as in Fig. 79.

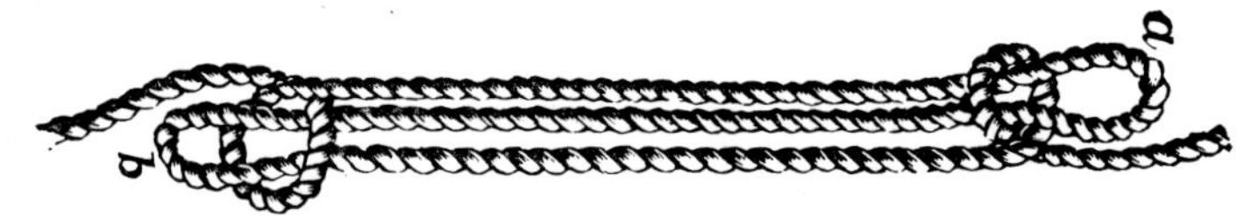

Fig. 79.

To render it still more dependable, the bights *a* and *b* may be seized or toggled to the standing parts as in Figs. 80 and 81.

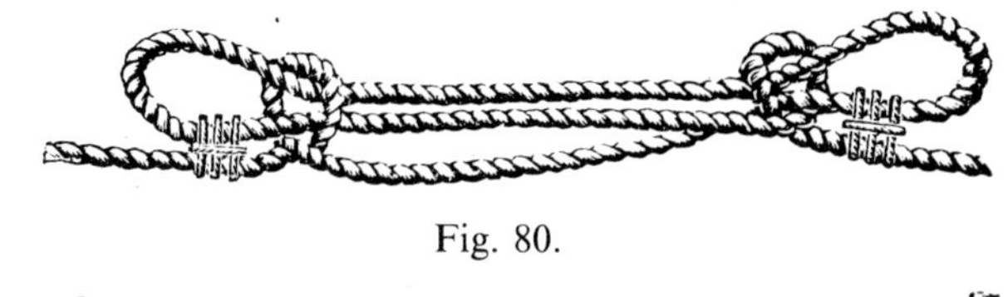

Fig. 80.

Fig. 81.

A Catspaw is formed in a rope to make a temporary loop for hooking on the block of a tackle. First throw back a bight as in Fig. 82.

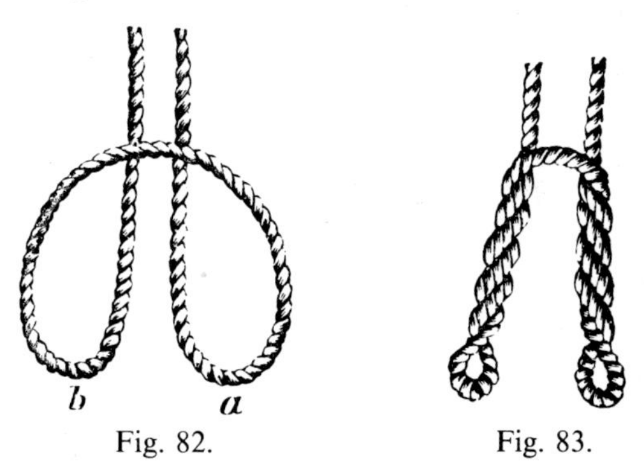

Fig. 82. Fig. 83.

Then taking hold of *a* and *b* in either hand twist them up as in Fig. 83; bring together the two eyes *a* and *b* and hook in the tackle.

Man Harness Hitch.—This forms a loop in a rope without using the ends. Throw a loop (Fig. 84), letting the

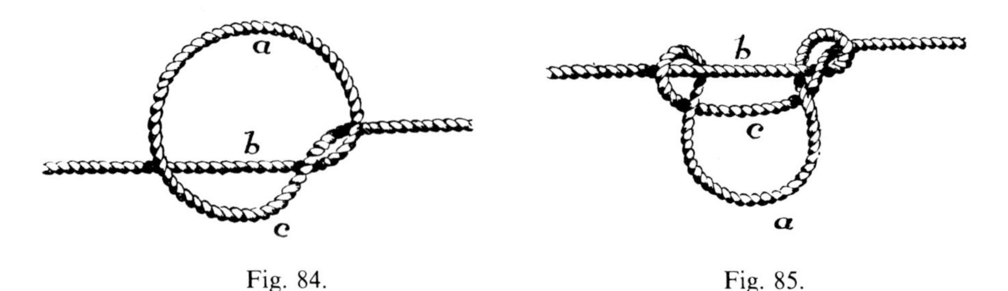

Fig. 84. Fig. 85.

ring *a* be at least as big as the final loop is to be. Pass loop *a* up between *b* and *c* and work it to shape (Fig. 85).

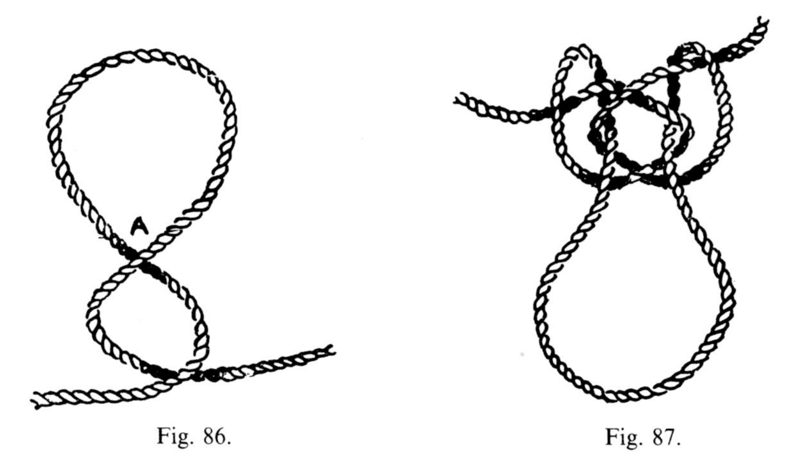

Fig. 86. Fig. 87.

Man Harness Hitch (Alternative form).—Form a bight and twist it twice on its axis (Fig. 86). Hold the crossing *A*, then take the head of the bight down over the rest of the knot and up through the loop below crossing *A* (Fig. 87).

KNOTS, BENDS AND HITCHES FOR UNITING ROPES.

Reef Knot.—The common knot for joining rope, but only to be recommended when the knot will bear against something. Twist the two ends together (Fig. 88), then twist them again, so that they lie alongside the standing parts (Fig. 89). If they are twisted the other way, they will lie across, forming an insecure granny knot.

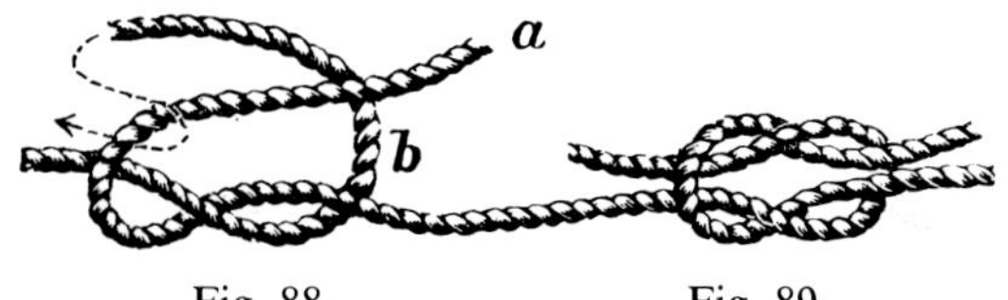

Fig. 88. Fig. 89.

Sheet or Common Bend.—This is used for joining ropes when the knot is unsupported, particularly when they are of different sizes. Form a bight in one rope (Fig. 90). This should be the thicker if they are of different sizes. Pass the end of the second rope up through the eye *a*, around *b*, then around *c* and under itself across *b* (Fig. 91). If there is a considerable difference in sizes or the ropes are wet, take the end around a second time to make a double sheet bend (Fig. 92).

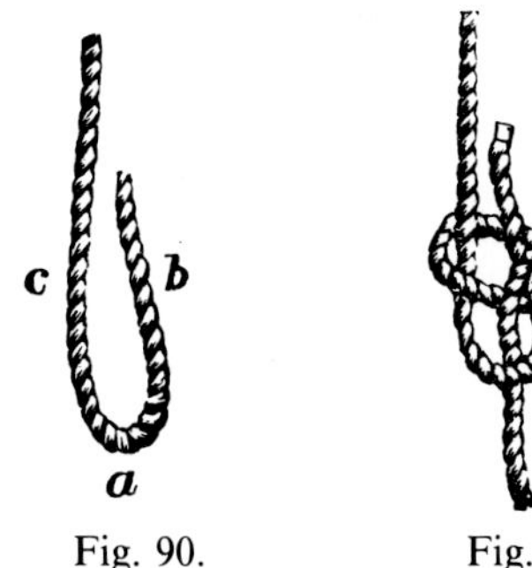

Fig. 90. Fig. 91. Fig. 92.

Carrick Bend.—Where large ropes have to be joined, this is preferable to many other knots. It also forms the foundation of several fancy knots. Cross the end of one rope over its standing part (Fig. 93). Take the end of the other rope

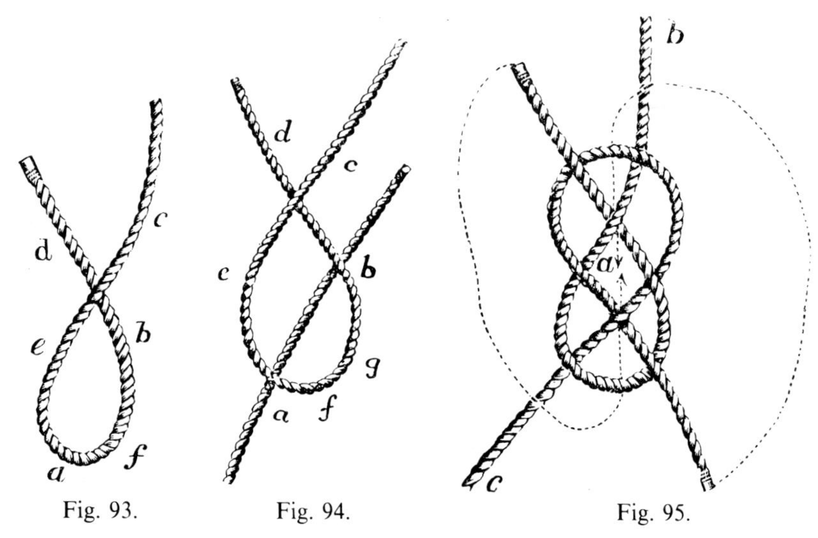

Fig. 93. Fig. 94. Fig. 95.

under parts *a* and *b* (Fig. 94), then alternately over *c*, under *d*, over *e*, under its own standing part and over *f*. This should result in every part being held against the other parts (Fig. 95) without going through a loop. The ends should come out on opposite sides of the knot, and if the knot is being used to join large ropes, the ends should be seized back to the standing parts.

Diamond Knot.—This is a fancy knot developed from the Carrick Bend, and it is often used in making lanyards.

Make a Carrick Bend, with long ends (Fig. 95). Take the ends around and up through the space *a*. Bring the standing parts *b* and *c* together and work up the parts as tight as possible. The knot may be doubled by following round again. If parts *a* and *b* are part of the same bight the knot forms a loop for the end of a lanyard (Fig. 96).

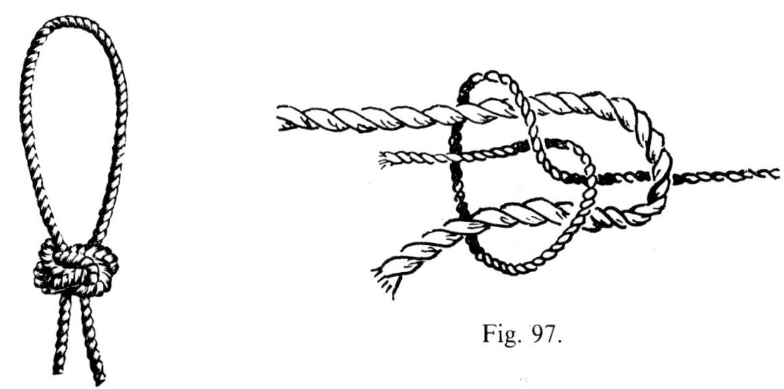

Fig. 97.

Fig. 96.

Binder Turn.—This is a variation on the sheet, in which both ends point the same way—an advantage when the knot has to pass through machinery (Fig. 97).

Weaver's Knot.—This differs from the sheet bend mainly in the method of tying, although in this version the ends come out on opposite sides, instead of the same side, which is usual in a sheet bend. It is used to join a broken thread without stopping the loom. The two ends are laid together and a loop of one thrown over the crossing (Fig. 98A). The end of the other is brought down through the loop

(Fig. 98B), and the standing parts pulled to shape the knot (Fig. 98C).

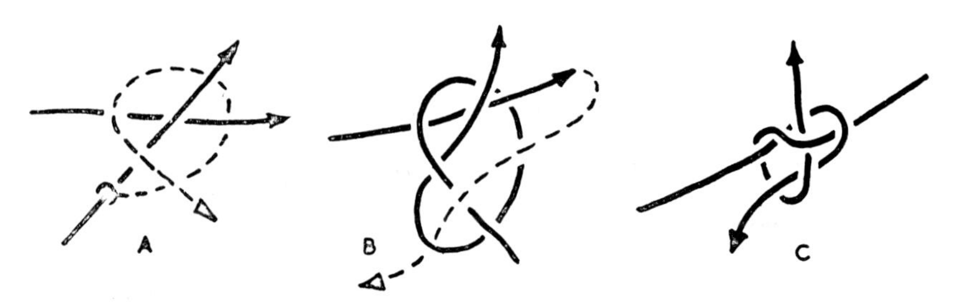

Fig. 98.

Double Overhand or Thumb Knots.—Fig. 99 shews the "Sliding Double Overhand Knot". Put an overhand knot on

Fig. 99.

one rope, then pass the other rope through the knot and put an overhand knot on it and round the first rope. Haul tight.

Fig. 100 shews the interlaced "Double Thumb Knot". Put an overhand knot on one rope (shewn shaded) then pass

Fig. 100.

the other rope through the knot and "follow round" the knot on the first rope as indicated by the dotted line.

These knots form probably the strongest knots for joining light lines as there is no sharp "nip". They are, however, very difficult to undo.

Constrictor Knot.—This is a knot which is very useful for holding secure a number of strands, as when making "fancy" knots. Of course seizings may be used but they take time to tie. The knot shewn has proved in everyway adequate. So long as it is tied over a convex surface it will not slip. It draws up easily, has a ratchet-like grip and is the most secure of all binding knots Fig. 101.

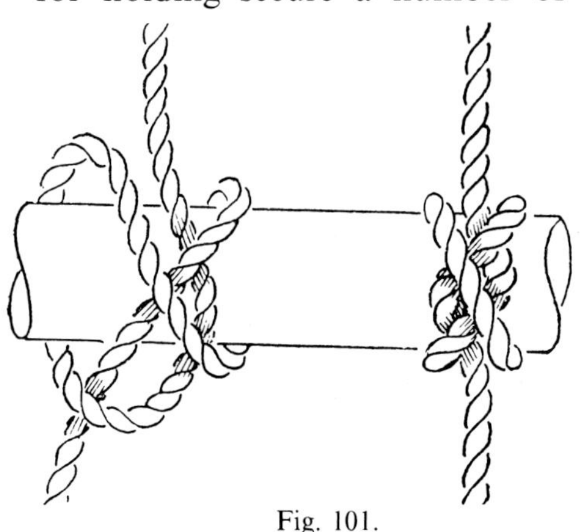

Fig. 101.

KNOTS FORMED ON ROPES BY THEIR OWN STRANDS.

Spunyarn or Marline Knot.—Take the ends of the spunyarn or marline, split them into two and crutch them together as shewn in Fig. 102.

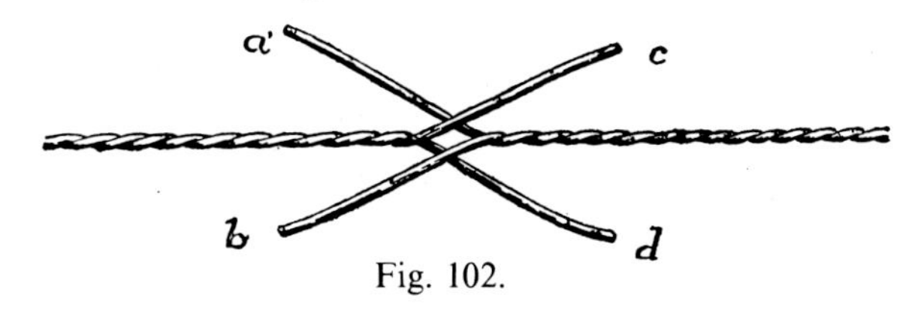

Fig. 102.

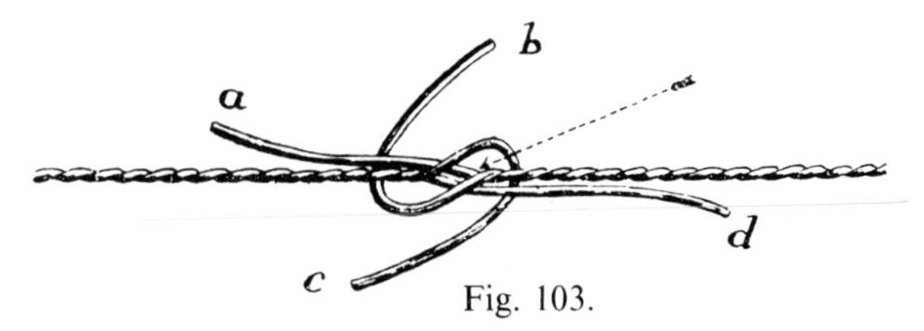

Fig. 103.

Then take strand *c* right round over the standing part and strand *b* round under the standing part as shown in Fig. 103. Knot them with a single knot in front where indicated by the arrow and draw tight.

The ends may then be trimmed off.

Although the next series of knots are generally known as "Fancy Knots" they are by no means merely ornamental, many of them playing important parts in the standing rigging of a ship.

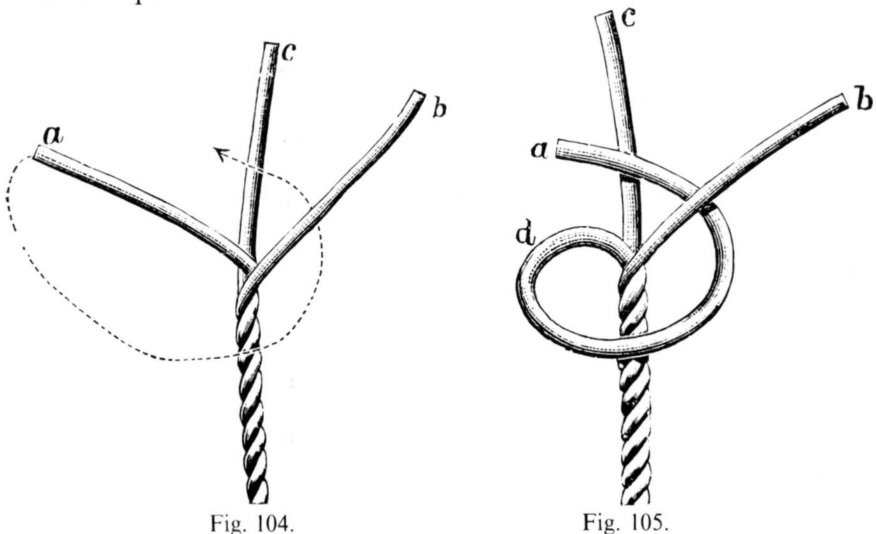

Fig. 104. Fig. 105.

To Form a Wall Knot.—First Unlay the rope so that the strands appear as in Fig. 104.

Holding the rope with the left hand, with the right lead strand *a* in the direction indicated by the dotted line, viz., under strand *b* and up between strands *b* and *c* (Fig. 105).

Then with strand *b* form a similar loop, enclosing strands *a* and *c*, and bringing the end of strand *b* up between *a* and *d* (Fig. 106).

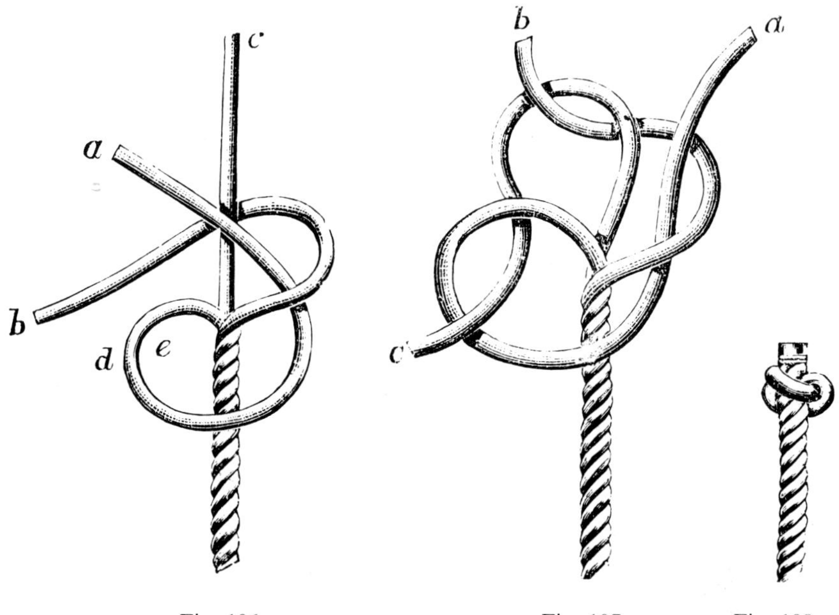

Fig. 106. Fig. 107. Fig. 108.

Now with strand *c* form a similar loop, enclosing strands *b* and *a* by leading the end of strand *c* up through the loop *e* in stand *a* (Fig. 107).

Finally, work all parts well taut, whip the ends of the strands together and cut off short (Fig. 108).

NOTE.—When Wall Knots are being used to make Shroud Knots (see Figs. 139 to 143) they ought to be made against the lay of the rope.

A Double Wall Knot is formed by allowing each strand to follow its lead as given in a Single Wall Knot, opening out the first loops again with a pricker sufficiently for the purpose. The three strands are as before bought up in the centre and cut off short after whipping them together. This knot is also known as a Stopper Knot.

A "Double Wall Knot", double crowned, was used on the ends of stoppers and shank painters. It was sometimes called a "Rose Knot".

Continuous Wall Knotting.—This is used to cover ropes, chest handles, etc. To make it, the requisite number of lengths of spunyarn or other suitable stuff are stoppered

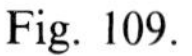

Fig. 109.

Fig. 110.

round the rope to be covered and are worked round it, one Wall Knot after another (Fig. 109). The same process can be carried out with a thin heart to form a plait, but continuous walling without any heart is not satisfactory as it is impossible to keep the "rounds" close together. A plait can be made by using a Wall Knot and a Crown Knot alternately (see Fig. 110).

Fig. 111.

Fig. 112.

A Crown Knot is formed by interlacing the strands in a similar manner to a Wall Knot, but the strands are successively led *over* each other instead of under. Its construction will be easily followed in Fig. 111.

Double crowning is done by following round each strand again alongside its first lead.

Continuous Crowning can be used to cover a rope. To make it, the requisite number of spunyarns or other suitable stuff are stoppered on to the rope to be covered and are worked round it, one Crown Knot after another (Fig. 112).

The same process can be carried out without a heart so as to form a plait. If all the crowns are made in one direction then a "Spiral Plait" is formed as shewn in Fig. 113, and if the crowns are made to the right and left alternately one gets a chain effect, like Fig. 114.

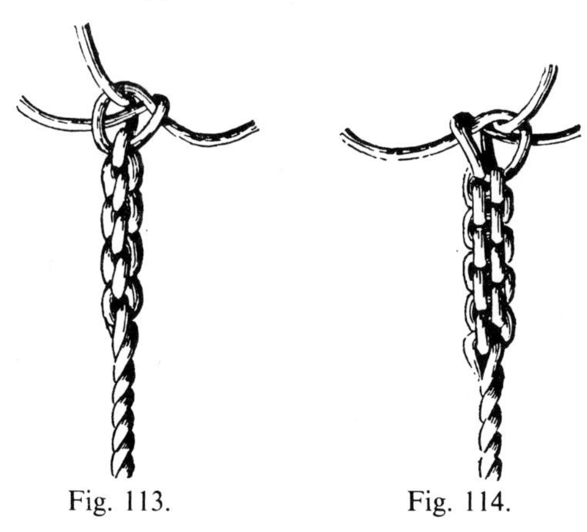

Fig. 113. Fig. 114.

A Manrope Knot is made by first forming a wall and then crowning it (Fig. 115).

Fig. 115.

Then follow round the wall again, and lastly, follow round the crown, when the finished knot will appear as in Fig. 116.

Fig. 116.

Stopper Knot.—A knot formed by making a crown first and then a wall, and afterwards following round the crown and wall again is the "Stopper Knot". It is very similar in appearance when finished to a "Manrope Knot".

Tack Knot.—The "Tack Rope" was made tapered where it passed through the clew of the sail. The Tack Knot is a Double Wall Knot, double crowned. This brings the strands out near the top of the knot. The strands are then tucked again, downwards and following the walling strands, thus bringing them out at the bottom of the knot. They were then laid down along the rope, scraped taper, and marled down. (Fig. 117).

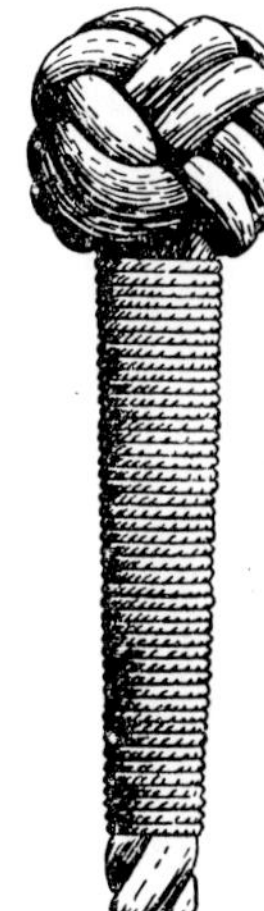

Fig. 117.

Strop Knot.—This is shown made with four strands. (Fig. 118).

Note.—Many knots can be made with loops of cord instead of with single cords. This knot is illustrated as made with loops.

Begin by making a Crown Knot and then make a Wall Knot and bring out the loop ends as shown.

Fig. 118.

Rose Knot.—First make a Wall Knot. Then make a Crown Knot. Then follow round the Wall Knot.

Then follow round the Crown Knot and tuck the ends down through the centre of the knot.

Fig. 119. Fig. 120.

Then make a Wall Knot, which brings the ends pointing upwards.

Then make a Diamond Knot. Follow round the Diamond Knot and tuck the ends of the strands up through the centre of the knot (Fig. 119).

Note.—The ends may then be cut off as shewn in Fig. 120, or they may be stoppered together as shewn in Fig. 119. The name given to this is a Chair Knot.

A Single Matthew Walker.—To make this knot, commence similarly to a wall, but pass the first strand *a* under both *b* and *c*, as in Fig. 121

Then pass *b* under both strands *c* and *a*, and bring up through the loop first formed by a (Fig. 122).

Similarly pass *c* under *a* and *b*, and bring up through the loops first formed by *a* and *b* (Fig. 123).

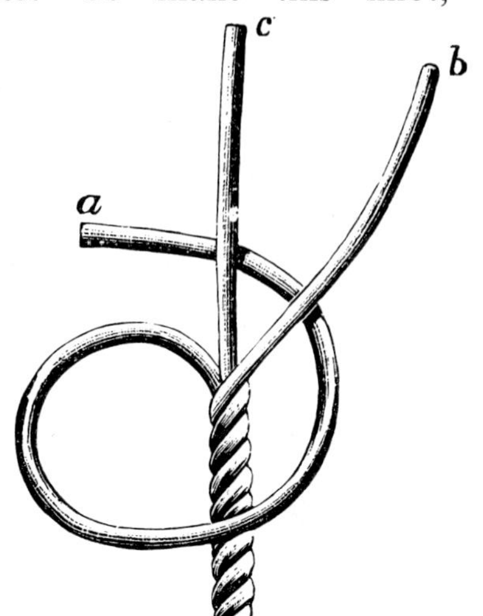

Fig. 121.

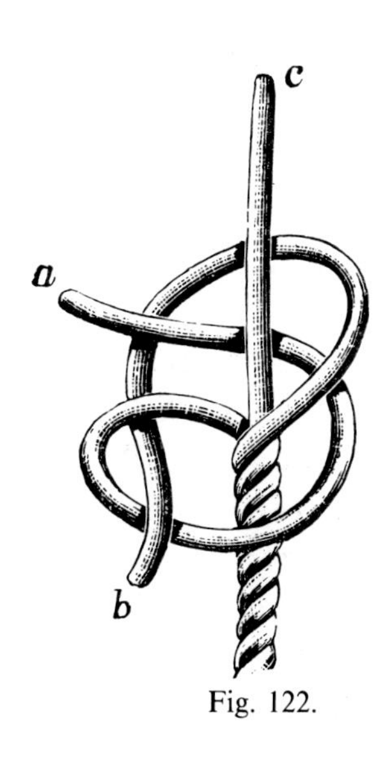

Fig. 122.

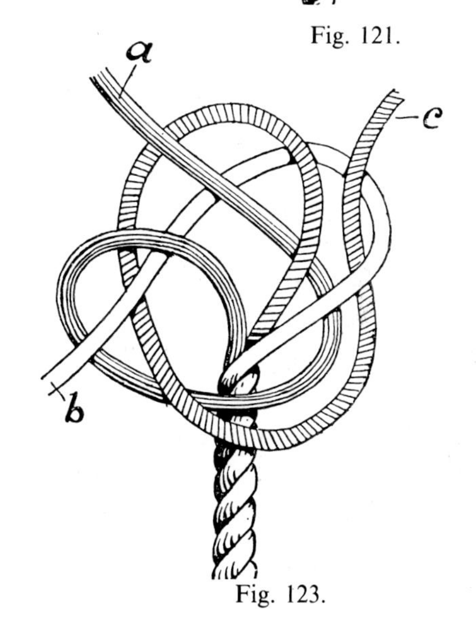

Fig. 123.

A Double Matthew Walker will be easily learnt if you notice the difference between a "Single Matthew Walker" and a Wall Knot.

In the Wall Knot you will have noticed that each strand is simply interlaced with the strand immediately on its right coming up through the loop formed by this second strand.

In the "Single Matthew Walker" each strand interlaces the two strands to its right, coming up through the loop of the third stand.

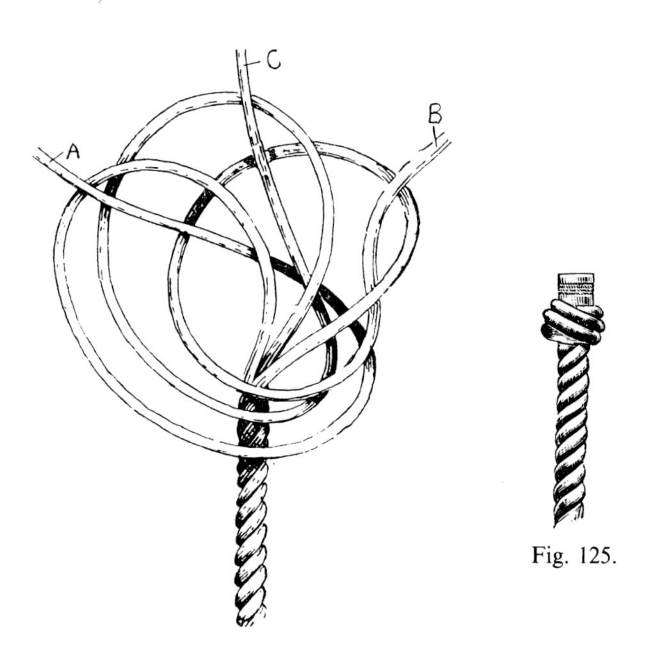

Fig. 125.

Fig. 124.

Another evolution in the same order brings us to the "Double Matthew Walker". It is formed, as will be seen by carefully following Fig. 124, by making each strand contain in its own loop the other two strands and *its own* end, that is, each strand leads up through its own bight after interlacing the other two. When worked taut and finished off, it will appear as in Fig. 125.

The knot is in fact a glorified Thumb Knot in that each strand is thumb knotted and interlaced with the other strands. This knot seems to be universally used on the end of rigging lanyards; it will not slip or capsize.

A Single Diamond Knot.—This is another method of forming the knot shown in Fig. 98 which in that case was formed by the two ends of the same rope.

To form it on a rope by its own strands, unlay the rope to the place where it is desired to form the knot, and as after the knot is made the strands will have to be laid up again, try to preserve the original lay in the strands as much as possible. Now bring each of the three strands down alongside the standing part of the rope, thus forming three bights, and hold them thus with the left hand. Take the first strand *a* (Fig. 126) and, putting it over the next, *b*, bring it up through the bight of the third strand *c*.

Take the end of the second strand over the third and up the bight of the first. The last strand is brought through over the first and up through the bight of the second. Haul taut, and lay the rope up again. Fig. 127 shows the loops in their places with the ends through them before they are hauled taut. Fig. 128 gives the knot finished.

For a double diamond we first make a single diamond, the ends are then made to follow the lead of the single knot through two single bights, the ends coming out on top of the

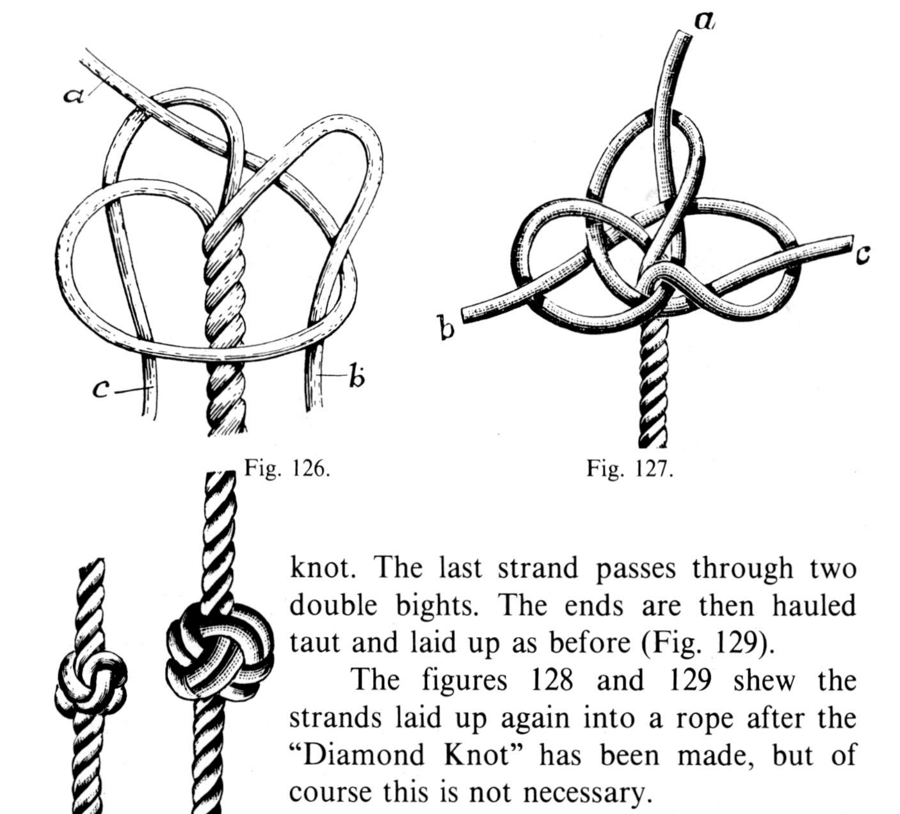

Fig. 126.

Fig. 127.

knot. The last strand passes through two double bights. The ends are then hauled taut and laid up as before (Fig. 129).

The figures 128 and 129 shew the strands laid up again into a rope after the "Diamond Knot" has been made, but of course this is not necessary.

Fig. 128. Fig. 129.

Sennit Knot.—Commence by making a Diamond Knot, then follow round only half way with each strand as shown in Fig. 130. Then instead of continuing to follow round, take each strand over the first crossing strands and under the next crossing strands as shown in Fig. 131.

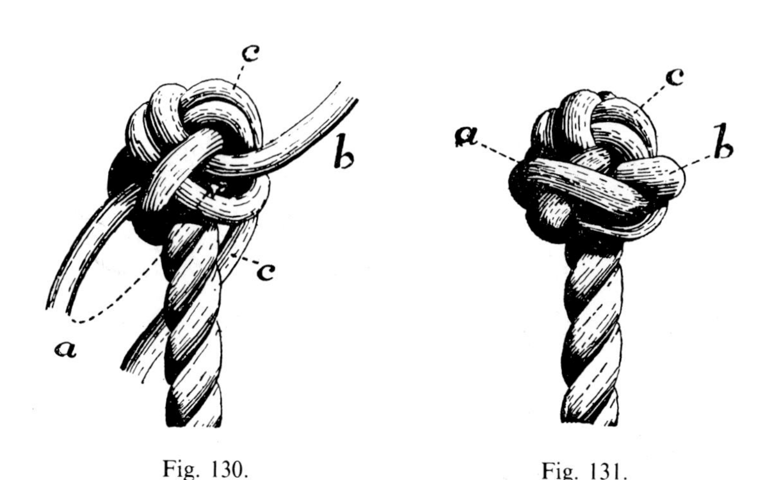

Fig. 130.

Fig. 131.

Sennit Knot (another form).—A better form of the Sennit Knot than that shewn in Figs. 130 and 131 is made as follows.

Begin by making a Diamond Knot. Then follow round, tucking each strand so that it comes below the strand it is following (Fig. 132).

Now tuck each strand upwards over two strands where they cross and under two strands where they cross. This will bring all the strands out in the centre of the knot. The ends are then whipped (Fig. 133).

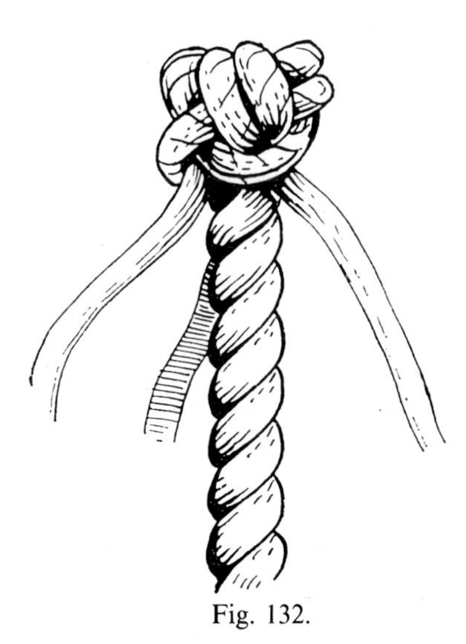

Fig. 132.

Fig. 133.

Diamond Hitching or Continuous Diamond Knotting.—Is sometimes used for covering rope. To make it, the requisite number of spunyarns on other suitable stuff are stoppered round the rope to be covered and are formed into one "Diamond Knot" after another as shown in Fig. 134.

Fig. 134.

A Plait can be make by making a "Diamond Knot" and "Crown Knot" alternately as in Fig. 135.

When using a number of strands it is difficult to manipulate them. A good method is to lay back the strands along the rope and pass a turn of twine round them. Then draw out a loop on each strand. The necessary tucks can easily be made and the twine removed.

Fig. 135.

Long Diamond Knot.—Begin by unlaying the rope and crowning end. Then work a Diamond Knot on the rope, but with the knot reversed, that is, so that when the knot is tied the strands are lying down along the rope instead of being at the top of the knot and clear of the rope, which is the ordinary way (see Fig. 136). This is the tricky bit of the work. It will be found best to form the knot well down the rope and, after it is formed, to work it out to the end near the crown.

Fig. 136.

Then work another Diamond Knot in the usual way but left handed. This brings the strands out in the middle of the knot as shown in Fig. 137.

Fig. 137.

Follow the strands round in the usual way. Fig. 138 shows this done in two tucks, but three tucks can be made by continuing to follow round.

Fig. 138.

Shroud Knot.—The "Shroud Knot" was used for repairing a shroud when it had been shot away in action. It requires less stuff than a splice and is more rapidly executed. Each rope is unlaid the necessary length, and they are then clutched together. A Wall Knot is then formed round each rope with the strands of the other (Fig. 139), but the Wall Knots must be laid against the lay of the rope. That is, if the rope is hawser or shroud-laid, the strands must be laid towards the left when forming the Wall Knots, and if the rope is cable-laid, the strands must be laid towards the right when forming the Wall Knots. The figure shows hawser or shroud-laid rope.

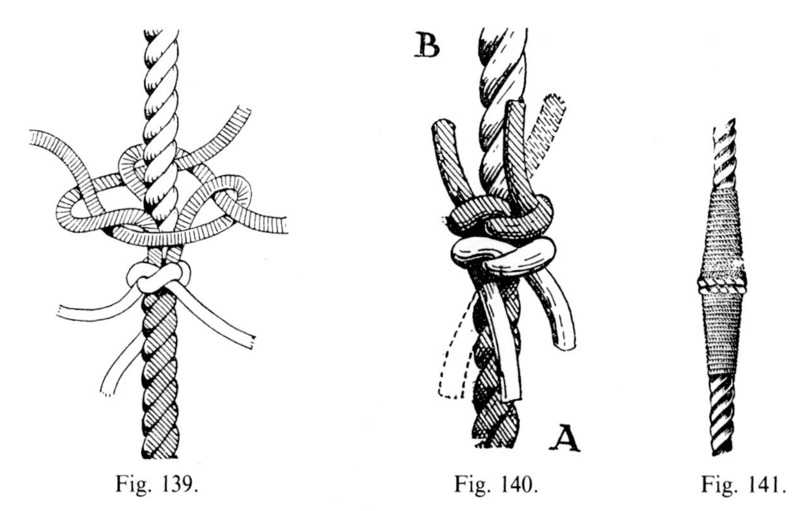

Fig. 139. Fig. 140. Fig. 141.

The completed knot is shown in Fig. 140, but to make a neat job the ends should be marled and served as in Fig. 141.

French Shroud Knots.—These knots were used for the same purpose as the Shroud Knot.

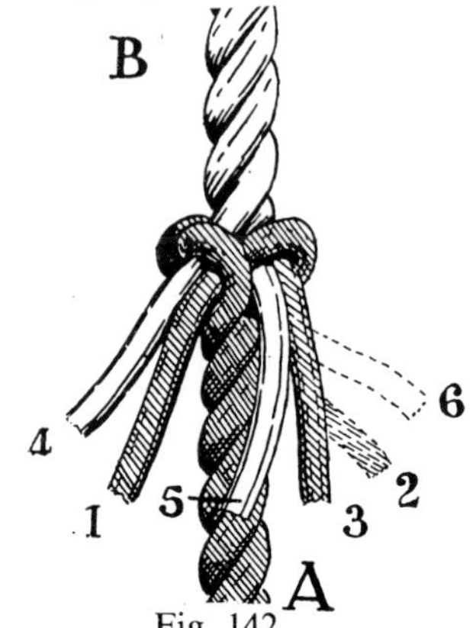

Fig. 142.

The first variety is made by unlaying the strands of the ropes to be joined and marrying them. Then cast a Crown Knot with strands 1, 2, 3, of rope *A* round rope *B* (left hand for hawser-laid rope as in Fig. 142, or right handed for cable-laid rope).

In the same way cast a Crown Knot with strands 4, 5, 6, of the other rope *B* round rope *A* when the knot will appear as in Fig. 143.

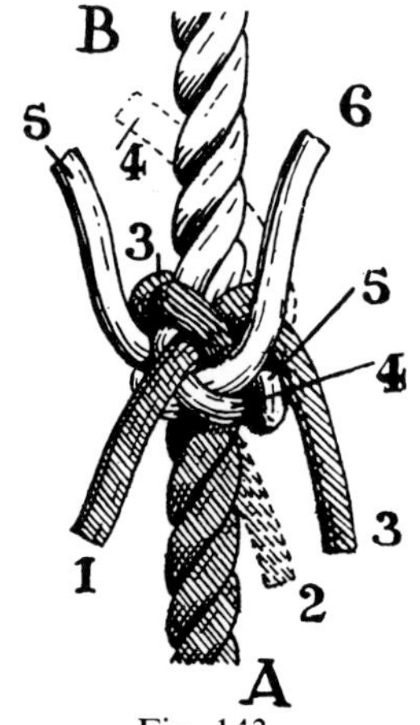

Fig. 143.

The strands may then be scraped and marled down.

The second variety of the French Shroud Knot is made in the same way except that the strands of one rope are tied in a Crown Knot and the strands of the other rope in a Wall Knot. This results in all the strands pointing the same way.

Spritsail Sheet Knot.—This is a knot formed on the two ends of the spritsail sheet block strop. The block was made with large cheeks through which were bored holes running longitudinally. The two ends of the strop were passed through these holes and then the knot was made on them. The block was thus held in the loop. When in use the knot was passed through the clew of the spritsail. A seizing was put on between the block and the knot. The block is omitted from the figures.

A Spritsail Sheet Knot.—Unlay both ends of the rope, pass them through the holes in the cheeks of the block, and bring the two standing parts of the rope together as in Fig. 144.

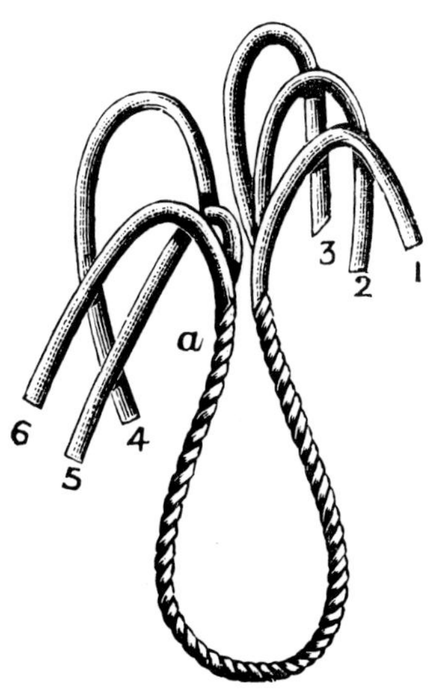

Fig. 144.

Grasping both parts of the rope at *a*, with the six strands form a Wall Knot, that is, by passing 1 under 2, 2 under 3, 3 under 4, 4 under 5, 5 under 6, and 6 under the loop formed by 1.

This would appear too confusing if shown in a diagram, but the knot is very easily made in practice.

Now lay any opposite two of the strands across the top in an *opposite direction*, and crown by passing the other four, each in turn, alternately over and under these two.

Each of the six strands will then come out leading in a downward direction alongside the strands forming the first walling, as shown in Fig. 145, which shows the knot at this stage looked at from the top.

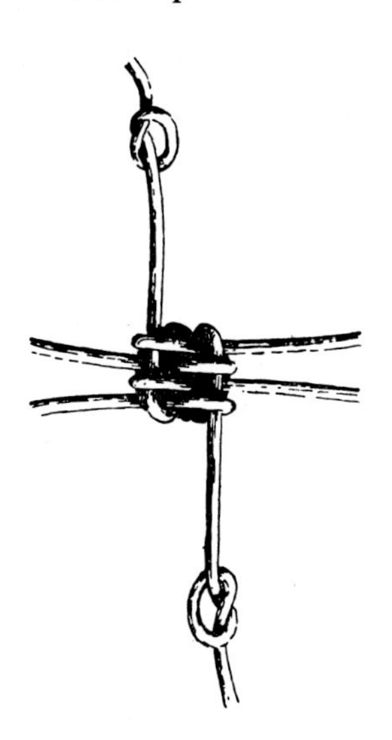

Fig. 145.

It will be noticed that six of the strands in the crown four strands run "over one and under one", and that the remaining two strands (indicated by Thumb Knots) run "over one, under one, over one, under one". This must be noted because unless great care be exercised with the second crowning confusion will result.

Now follow round the walling again, when the strands will come through in an upward direction, each alongside a strand of the first crowning.

Follow through the crowning for the second time. The best way to do this is to begin by tucking the two strands that go "over one, under one, over one, under one" and mark them by tying an overhand knot on each. Then tuck the remaining four strands. Cut off the strands short, when a handsome and useful stopper knot will result, as shown in Fig. 146.

Fig. 146.

Footrope Knot.—This knot was used on the footropes or "horses" to prevent the men's feet from slipping. It looks, when finished, like a "Turk's Head Knot", but as it is worked through the rope it is not liable to slip along it.

Pass two pieces of line through the rope as shown in Fig. 147.

Fig. 147.

Work the four ends into a Diamond Knot as shewn in Fig. 148.

Fig. 148.

Follow round once or twice and cut off the ends.

The knot can be made with any convenient number of ends.

Long Footrope Knot.—Form a Footrope Knot as shown in Fig. 148, then, turning the rope end for end form another Footrope Knot but laid left-handed as shown in Fig. 149. The ends of the strands come out in the centre of the knot.

Follow right round and the result is a very handsome and useful collar as shewn in Fig. 150, where the following round has been done twice, *i.e.* three tucks in all.

Fig. 149.

Fig. 150.

Star Knot.—This is one of the most complicated of the fancy knots but each stage is quite simple in itself.

The knot is shewn made with six strands and the rope should be whipped at the place to which it has been unlaid.

Commence as shewn in Fig. 151. The first stage, finished, is shown in Fig. 152.

In Fig. 153 the part of the knot already made is only indicated to make this second stage clearer. The strands are worked into a crown, but backwards, or left-handed (Fig. 153). This concludes stage two.

Each strand is now tucked back under its own part as shewn in the two long strands in Fig. 154. This is the third stage. When this has been finished, the knot seen from the side will look like Fig. 155 and all the strands will leȧd up in the middle.

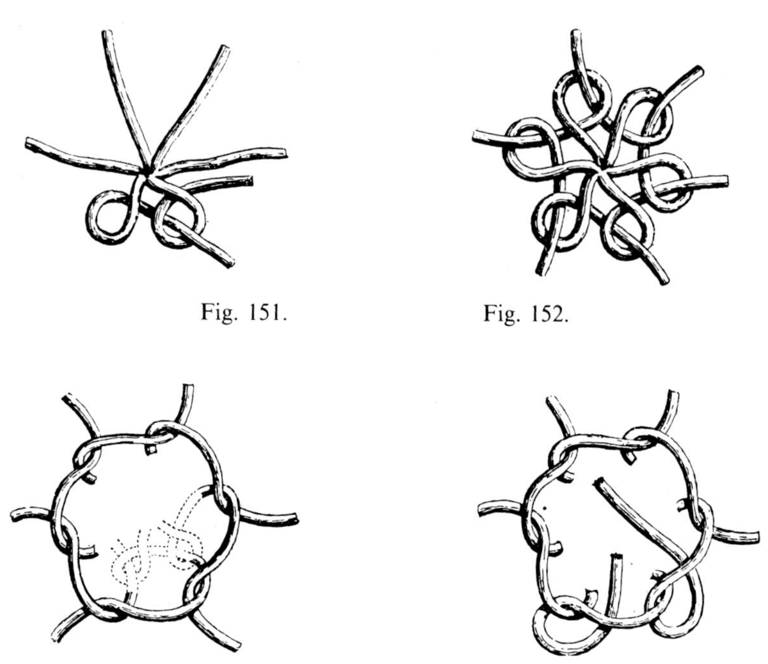

Fig. 151. Fig. 152.

Fig. 153. Fig. 154.

Each strand must now follow the lead of the part immediately on its right and be tucked down under two parts as shewn in Fig. 156, where two strands are shewn tucked and the path of a third stand indicated by the dotted line. When all the strands have been tucked the knot will look like

Fig. 157 and the strands come out on the underside of the knot. This completes the fourth stage.

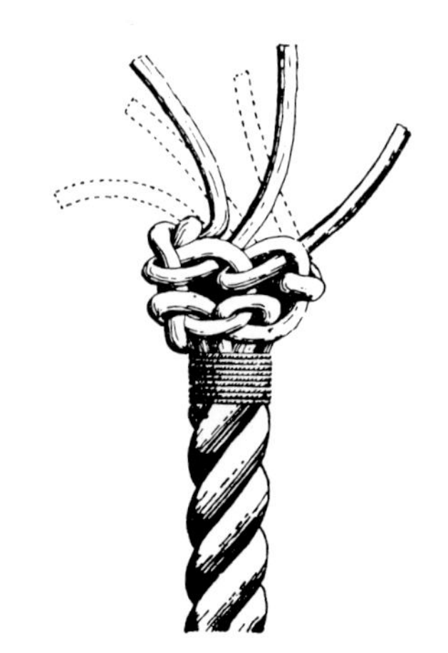

Fig. 155.

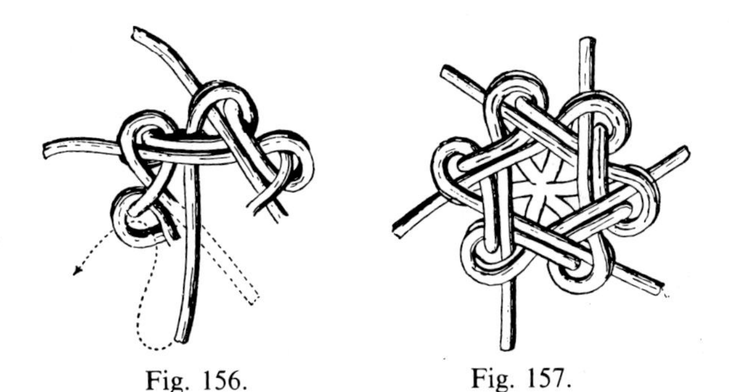

Fig. 156. Fig. 157.

Each strand is now taken following the neighbouring strand to the left and is tucked right through the knot and brought up through the centre. The strands may then be whipped and cut off. This is shown in Fig. 158.

Another finish to the knot is, instead of whipping the strands together and cutting off, make the strands into a crown. This will bring them pointing radially outwards.

Fig. 158. Fig. 159

Take each strand, turn it inwards over the crown, laying it between the strands of the crown, and tuck it right down through the knot. The strands are then cut off close to the bottom of the knot.

Fig. 159 shews this finish. The last strand has been tucked but not hauled tight.

Round Turn Knot.—This knot may be made with different numbers of strands. The figures shew the knot made with four strands and then a knot made with eight strands (Fig. 164).

Begin by making a Crown Knot (Fig. 160). Then make a Wall Knot (Fig. 161) towards the left, and round the bottom of the knot. This brings the strands pointing upwards.

Then make a Crown Knot towards the right, tucking the strands below the crown first made and of course below the next strand of the crown (Fig. 162).

Then lead each strand to the left and tuck it up through the centre of the knot (Fig. 163).

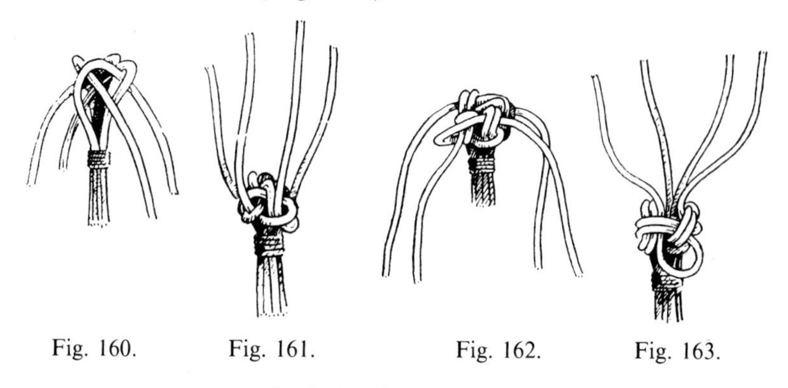

Fig. 160. Fig. 161. Fig. 162. Fig. 163.

Fig. 164.

Chequer Knot.—Used on the ends of man ropes, bell lanyards, etc. It may be made with any number of strands from four upwards. The figures shew 8 strands.

This knot may be finished in various ways; for instance, with Turk's Head, with Star Knot, with Round Turn Knot.

Chequer Knot with Round Turn Knot.—The knot is made round a heart, or core of spunyarn, etc.

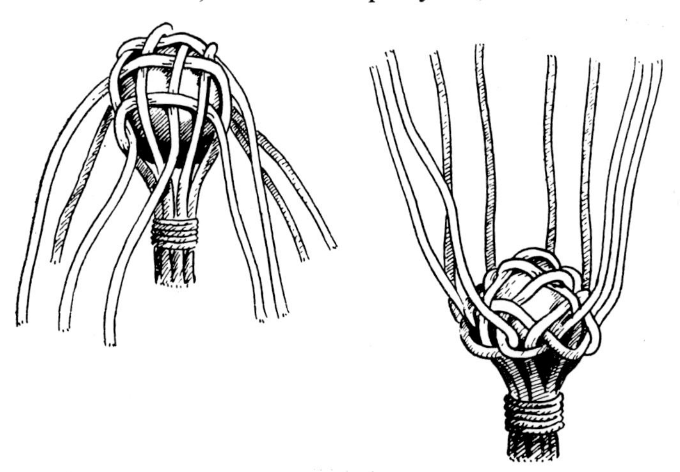

Fig. 165.—First Stage. Fig. 166.—Second Stage.

Begin by making a Crown Knot, left handed, over the heart, with the four alternate strands, say the even numbers. Then with the other four strands, the odd numbers, make a crown, right handed, and interlaced with the crown already made with the even number strands, as shewn in Fig. 165—First stage.

Then with all eight strands make a Wall Knot which

brings them pointing upwards as shown in Fig. 166—Second stage.

Then follow round, which will bring the knot to the form shewn in Fig. 167—Third stage.

The strands are now taken round to the right and tucked as shewn in Fig. 168—Fourth stage, and finished as Round Turn Knot.

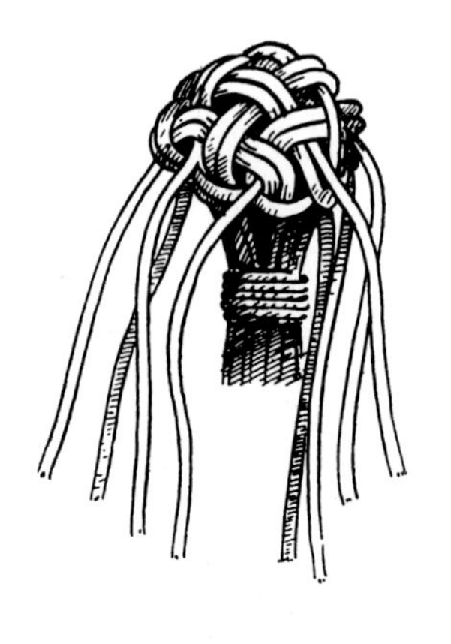

Fig. 167.—Third Stage.

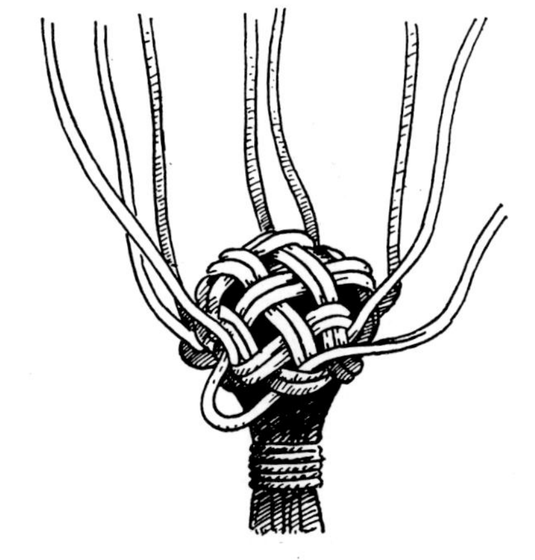

Fig. 168.—Fourth Stage.

Chequer Knot with Turk's Head.—After making the Chequer Knot as far as stage 3, Fig. 167, make a Wall Knot with all the strands as shewn in sketch. (Fig. 169—First stage)

Then form a Crown Knot as shewn in sketch. (Fig. 170—Second stage)

Follow round as shewn in sketch. (Fig. 171—Third stage).

Tuck the ends of the strands as shewn in sketch. (Fig. 172—Fourth stage).

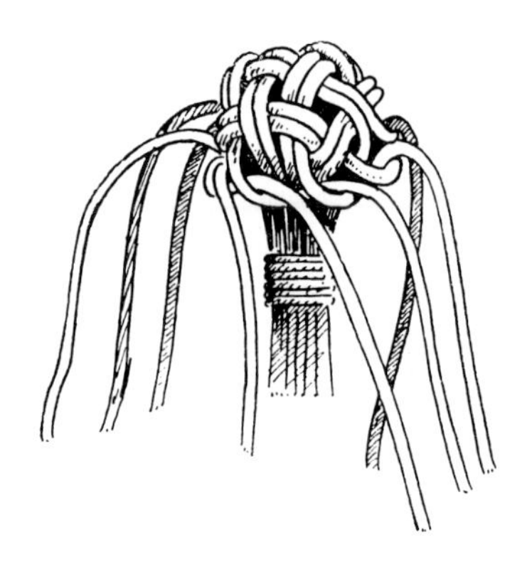

Fig. 169.—First Stage.

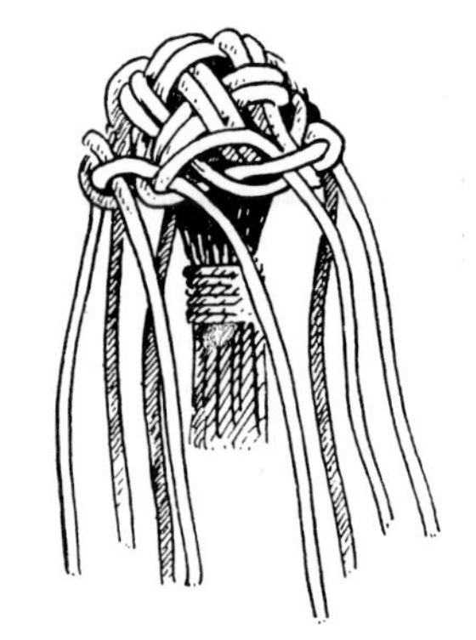

Fig. 170.—Second Stage.

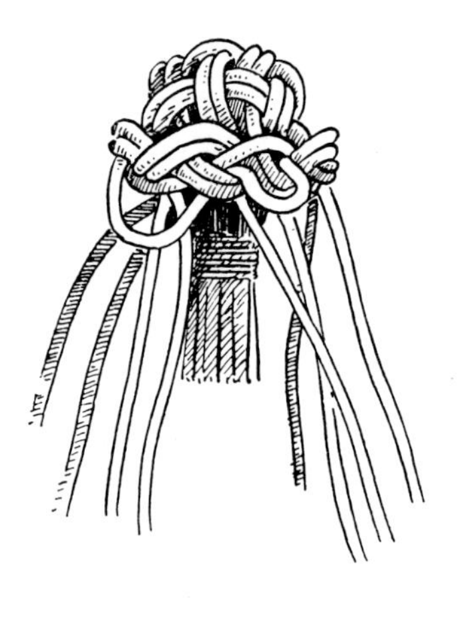

Fig. 171.—Third Stage.

Fig. 172.—Fourth Stage.

Chequer Knot with Star Knot.—This is made in a similar way to the Chequer Knot with Turk's Head except

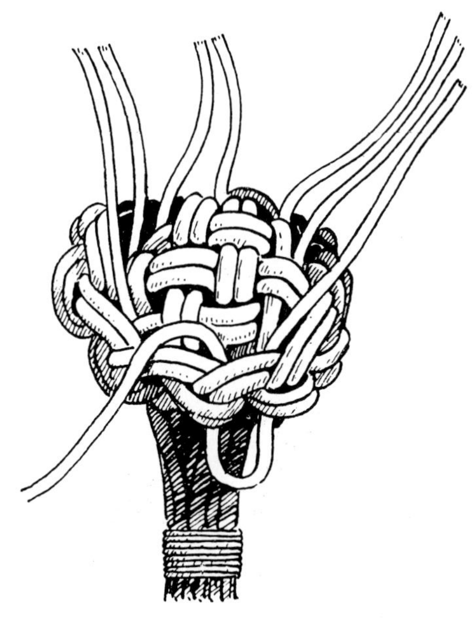

Fig. 173.

that a Star Knot is worked instead of a Turk's Head. Fig. 173 shews the completed knot. The ends of the strands would be cut off.

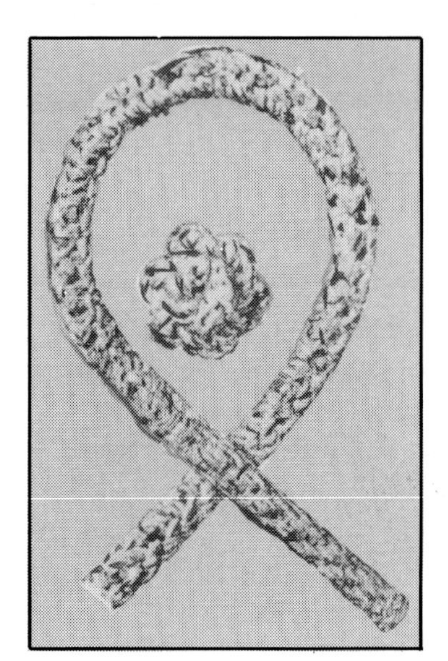

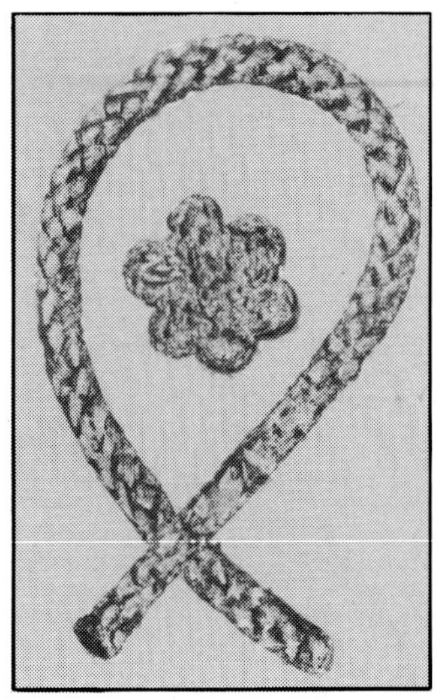

Fig. 174.

MAN ROPE—*Left.*—This was made of round sennit, using six strands and a heart of cotton rope. One end is spiral pointed, "Ron" finish and five-part Turk's head. The knot on the other end is a Star knot with a crown finish.

TILLER LINE—*Right.*—This is made of braided rope. One end is straight pointed. The knot on the other end is a Star Knot with whipped finish.

SPLICES.

Note.—If a short splice or eye splice is not served over after splicing, the ends of the strands, after splicing, should be halved and each half strand whipped to the half of the next strand; one half to the right, one half to the left.

Eye Splice.—An eye splice is formed by unlaying the end of a rope for a short distance, then turning the end back to form an eye, and tucking the separated strands into the standing part. Let the strands lie across the standing part approximately at right-angles to the lay of the standing part. Have two strands on top and one underneath. Lift a strand of the standing part with a spike, and tuck No. 2 strand under it (Fig. 175a). Lift the next strand and tuck No. 1 strand under it, going in where No. 2 comes out (Fig. 175b). Turn the loop over and lift the only strand of the standing

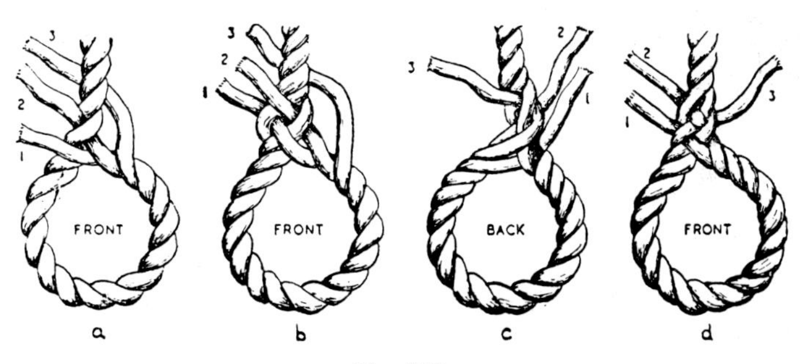

Fig. 175.

part which has no other under it, and insert No. 3. Notice its direction (175c).

Pull all the strands tight. This completes the first tuck. Take each strand in turn and "go over and under one", as No. 2 in Fig. 175d. Taper off by halving the strands before tucking the third time, and again halve them before the fourth tuck.

Sailmaker's Splice.—In a sailmaker's splice the strands are tucked with the lay of the rope. The tuck strands therefore each go round and round the same strand of the rope instead of going over and under alternate strands.

Another method is, to tuck the three strands from left to right, first round. Then they are all tucked to the left against the lay, over one and under one. Then each is tucked to the right round and under the same strand, to the left.

A Short Splice is used to join two ropes when not required to pass a through a block. Unlay the two ropes the required distance, and clutch them together as in Fig. 176; that is, so that the strands of one rope go alternately between the strands of the other.

Fig. 176.

Then tuck the strands of rope *a* into the rope *b* in a

similar manner to that described in an eye splice and similarly tuck the strands of *b* into *a* (Figs. 177 and 178).

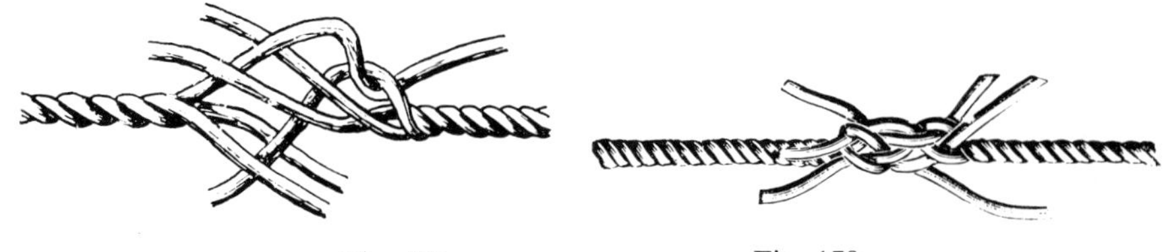

Fig. 177. Fig. 178.

A Cut Splice is made by laying two ropes in the position indicated in Fig. 179.

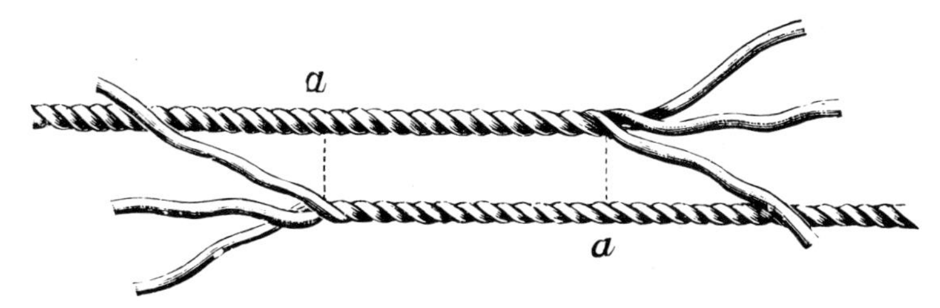

Fig. 179.

Leaving the ropes between *a a* to form an oblong loop, tuck the strands of one rope into the other as done in the eye splice. Splices are often wormed, parcelled, and served. Fig. 180 shows the cut splice after this treatment.

Fig. 180.

A Log-line Splice is a cut splice, but instead of allowing the loop to appear the two lines are twisted together.

A Long Splice is one of the most useful of splices, as it permits the rope to run through a block just the same as an unspliced rope. There are many ways of making a long splice but they differ only in detail. It used to be said that every ship had her own way of making long splices! This is one way:—

Unlay the ends of two ropes to a distance about four times the length used in a short splice—about 12 to 14 times the circumference of the rope is a good rule—and then clutch them together as if about to commence a short splice. Now unlay one strand for a considerable distance and fill up the gap thus caused by twisting in the strand opposite to it of the other rope. Then do the same with two more strands. Let the remaining two strands stay as they were first placed. The ropes will now appear as in Fig. 181. To finish off, tuck the

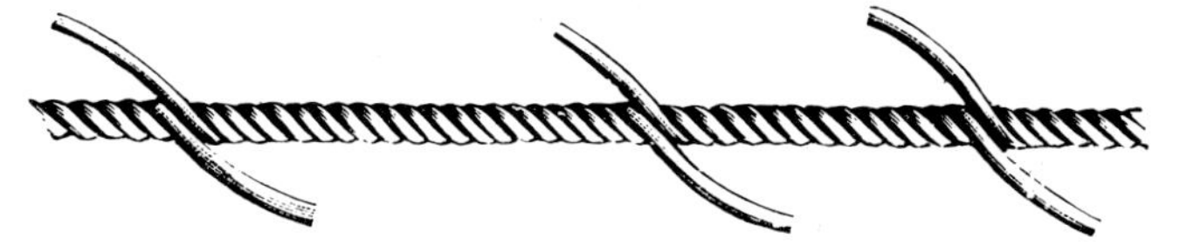

Fig. 181.

ends as in a short splice, but *with* the lay of the rope, that is, so that the tuck will continually take place around the same strand, and taper off gradually by reducing the yarns in the strand.

One variation is, before tucking the ends, half them and tuck each half round different strands. This makes a very smooth splice.

Another variation is to cast an Overland Knot on the two adjacent strands and tuck them as in a short splice, tapering off as usual.

To Splice an Eye in the Middle of a Rope.—At the place where the eye is be made, untwist the rope as shewn in Fig. 182. Continue doing this and the strands will twist on themselves as shewn in Fig. 183.

Fig. 182. Fig. 183.

When these ends are long enough, bend the rope into an eye and tuck the twisted strands as in an ordinary splice.

Note.—In the sketches only two strands are shown, the third strand being at the back.

Eye Splice Wormed and Collared.—This is a very smart eye splice. It may be used where the splice does not come close up to a block. It takes more rope than a common eye splice.

Begin as for an ordinary eye splice. When the first tuck has been made, separate four yarns of each strand and, with the remaining yarns, proceed to make a Sailmaker's Splice, tapering in the usual way by leaving out a yarn at intervals.

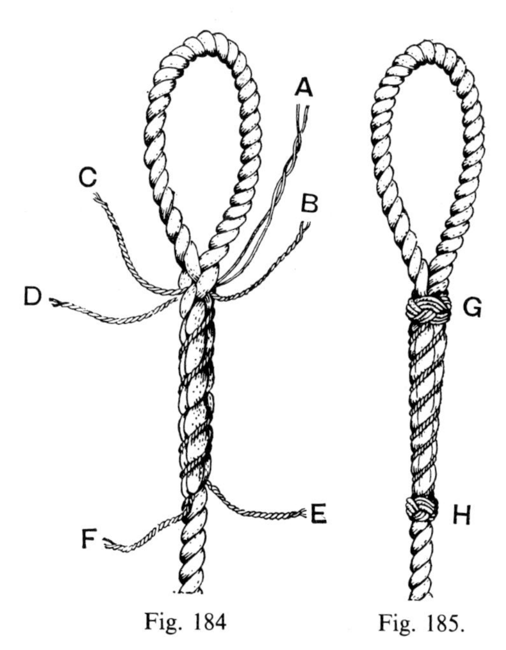

Fig. 184 Fig. 185.

Then lay up the yarns left out into two-yarn nettles. *A* shrews two yarns, and *B, C, D, E* and *F* shew two yarns each laid up into a nettle.

Take one nettle of each strand and lay it in as worming *E* and *F* shew two nettles laid in as worming.

At the end of the splice each worming nettle is tucked under a strand of the rope. (Fig. 184).

With these three nettles form a Footrope Knot.

Now take the three nettles left at the neck of the splice and form them into a Footrope Knot.

The completed splice is shewn in Fig. 185, *G* and *H* being the Footrope Knots.

Eye Splice, Single Tuck and Wall Knot.—Sometimes on the end of a rope an eye is required that must run close up to a block. An ordinary splice would tend to jam in the block so an "eye" is made with only one tuck of splicing and then a Wall Knot is cast round the rope and doubled (see Figs. 186 and 187).

Fig. 186.

Fig. 187.

Grafted Splice.—This was done by stopping on to the splice after it had been well beaten in a sufficient number of nettles and covering the splice with pointing or with coach whipping.

Back Splice.—This is used instead of whipping, on the end of a rope to prevent it from unlaying.

Unlay a short length ot the rope, crown the strands and then tuck them back along the rope in the same manner as when making a short splice.

Flemish Eye.—Unlay one strand *C* of the rope (Fig. 188)

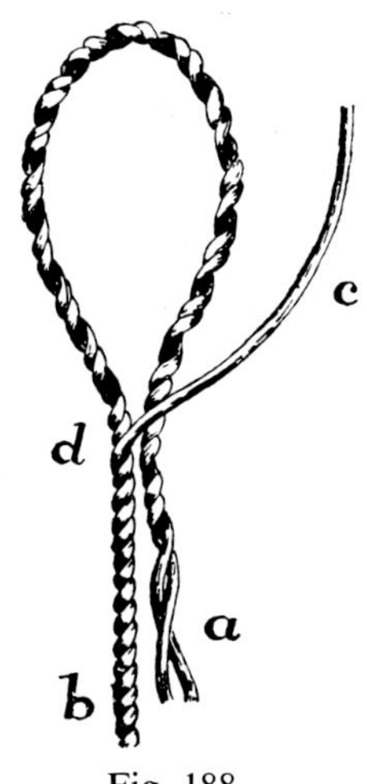

Fig. 188.

to a distance equal to the circumference of the desired eye and one half. Form the eye by placing the two strands which are not unlaid, *A*, alongside the standing part of the rope *B*.

Then lay stand *C* back into the space from which it was unlaid until it returns and lies in the fork *D*. All the strands are then unlaid, scraped down taper and marled or served down on *B*.

When working with four strand rope proceed as above with one strand, and when that strand has been laid round the eye carry out the same procedure with another strand but not with the strand adjacent to the one first used.

Chain Splice.—This is a splice used when splicing a rope through the end link of a chain.

The rope is unlaid as for an ordinary Eye Splice but for about twice the distance. One strand is then unlaid a farther distance equal to the length of the eye and one turn more. The remaining two strands are passed through the end link of the chain and turned round into the eye. One of them is now laid into the space left by the strand that was unlaid and that

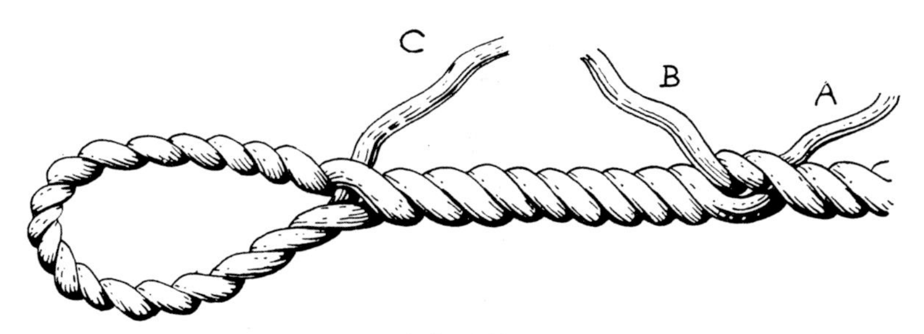

Fig. 189.

strand is farther unlaid and its space filled for a distance of about a foot. The two strands are then half-knotted and finished off as in a long splice (*A* and *B*). The remaining strand *C* is tucked as in an ordinary Eye Splice (Fig. 189).

A Drawing Splice.—This is a splice for cables. It is the best method of joining them in such a way that they will run through a hawse-hole. By this method also it is possible to take them apart again without damage.

A stop is put on each cable at about 3 fathoms from the end, but this depends on the size of the cable. The cables are then unlaid and stops are put on to each of the three ropes of which the cables are composed at about a fathom from the end.

These ropes are now unlaid and the strands are tapered and laid up again. In this way each of the three ropes of which the cables are composed is worked into a long taper.

The two cables are now married and short-spliced in the usual way. At each end of the splice a stout seizing is put on. Then the tapered ends are wormed round the cable, the ends are seized down and a seizing is put on halfway between the ends and the splice.

SPLICES OF ROPES OF THREE STRANDS INTO ROPES OF FOUR STRANDS.

A Short Splice.—After unlaying the ropes as far as necessary (and this means that the three strand rope must be unlaid for about twice the distance of the four strand rope) divide one of the strands of the three strand ropes into two. Then lay up the four strands thus made for a length that will take the tucks of the strands of the four strand rope. Crutch the ropes together and splice them.

A Long Splice.—Unlay the two ropes and crutch them in the usual way. Unlay one strand of three strand rope and lay in a strand of the four strand rope. Then unlay a strand of the four strand rope and lay in a strand of the three strand rope.

Then divide the remaining strand of the three strand rope into two unequal portions, one-third and two-thirds. The one-third portion is then half knotted with one of the two strands of the four strand rope that remain and the remaining two-thirds portion is laid into the space left by unlaying the fourth strand of the four strand rope. The ends are then knotted in the usual way for a Long Splice, tucked and cut off.

Mariner's Splice.—This is a long splice in cable-laid rope. It is made by unlaying the ends of the cables for a distance equal to six times the circumference. Then each of the ropes of which the cable was made is unlaid and married with the corresponding rope of the other cable. The places where the ropes are married are so arranged that the splices do not all come opposite each other. The three ropes of each cable are long-spliced into the corresponding ropes of the other cable. This is a difficult job and was looked upon as a test of skill.

A Grecian Splice.—This splice was sometimes used to repair standing rigging instead of a Shroud Knot because it made a neater join, but it takes more stuff and more time.

Begin by putting on a stop or whipping on both ropes at a distance from the ends about one and a half times what would be required for a Short Splice. Unlay the ends to the stop.

From the outside yarns of the strands lay up stout nettles, leaving about half the strand.

Lay up the strands again into a rope (leaving out the nettles of course) for a distance that will take one tuck each way of short splicing.

Marry the ropes and put in one tuck of splicing each way. From each strand take as many yarns as will make worming. Lay them in a worming and cut off the remaining yarns (Fig. 190).

Now take the nettles from one end of the splice *A* and lay them in a tight and even spiral over the splice, bringing them out between the nettles at *B,* and stopper them.

Then take the nettles at *B* and tuck them as in short

splicing with the *A* nettles, that is over one and under one, until the whole splice is covered with what is cross-pointing. The *A* nettles are now at the *B* end and the *B* nettles at the *A* end.

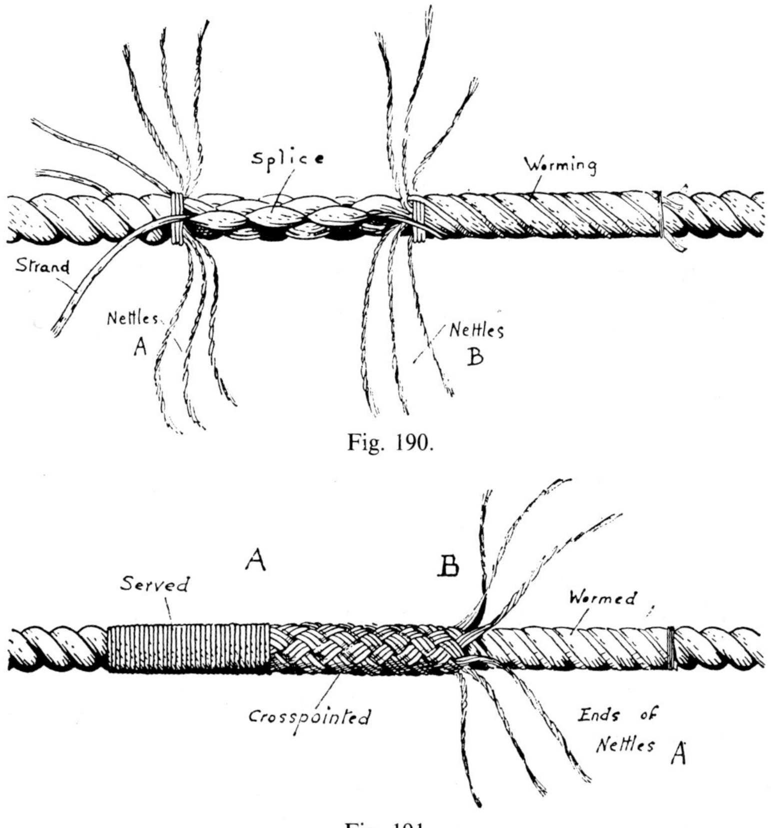

Fig. 190.

Fig. 191.

This cross-pointing should now be worked as tight as possible.

The ends of the nettles and the worming strands are now scraped taper and marled down and then served up to the cross-pointing which is over the splice (Fig. 191).

There are several methods of making the cross-pointing over the splice, besides the method given above.

One way is to take the nettles at *A* and cross-point them over the splice to *B*. Then the nettles at *B* are tucked so as to double them and come out at *A*.

Another way is to take the nettles from one end and lay them between the nettles at the other end, draw them tight and put on a stopper at the middle. Then tuck one lot as in short splicing up to the end of the splice, then take off the middle stopper and tuck the other lot of nettles up to the other end of the splice, getting in as many tucks as possible so as to tighten up the cross-pointing.

TAIL SPLICES
TO SPLICE HEMP AND WIRE ROPES TOGETHER.

Short Splice.—Unlay the end of the hemp rope as usual for a short splice.

Unlay the end of the wire rope for a like distance but unlay it in pairs of strands, that is, into three sets each of two strands. Cut off the heart.

Crutch the ropes together and tuck as for an ordinary short splicing using each pair of wire strands as a single strand. Serve all over.

Long Splice.—Unlay the end of the hemp rope as for a short splice and taper the ends of the strands.

Unlay the wire rope for a length equal to about 100 times the diameter of the wire rope.

Lay up three of the strands so unlaid into a "thin wire rope", having cut off the heart.

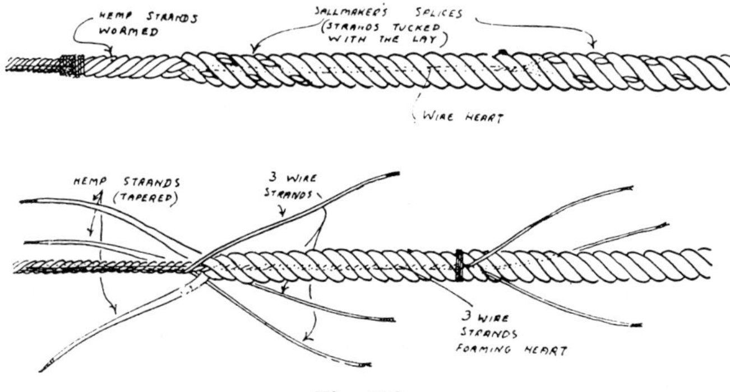

Fig. 192.

Crutch the hemp and the wire ropes together. Put on a stop of seaming twine and then lay the three strand "thin wire rope" into the hemp rope as a heart for a distance of about 80 diameters of the wire rope, and put on a stop of seaming twine.

Short-splice, sailmaker's fashion, the three strands of the wire rope at the crutch into the hemp rope. Or tuck the wire strands through the hemp rope strands two or three times. Cut off the ends.

Unlay the end of the "thin wire rope" heart of the hemp rope to the stopping and short splice, sailmaker's splice fashion (or tuck through the hemp strands as before) and cut off the ends.

Now take the tapered ends of the hemp rope strands and lay them tightly and smoothly along the wire rope, with the lay, and put on a stopping or seaming twine.

Parcel and serve over the splices and taper.

The hemp rope should be about four times the diameter of the wire rope.

Cable-Laid Ropes.—Require special methods on account of their construction and of their size.

A Ropemaker's Eye was formed on one end of a cable by the ropemaker. Two of the strands of a cable consist of a long rope doubled, thus forming an eye at one end. The third strand of the cable is turned round into an eye of the same size and its strands, instead of being tucked as in an ordinary eye splice, are wormed round the cable. The whole eye is then marled and served with good rope. The drawing shews the eye before worming (Fig. 193.

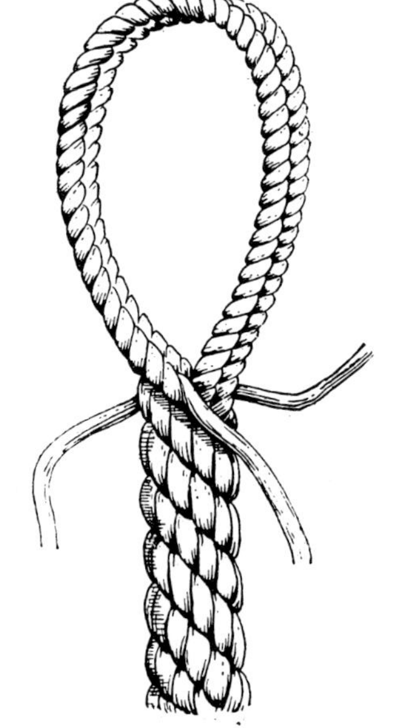

Fig. 193.

Admiral Elliott's Eye.—This is similar to the Ropemaker's Eye, but as there is no loop formed by the bight of the rope forming two of the strands, the ends of two strands are formed into a loop by a long splicing them

Fig. 194.

together. The third stand is then bent round and eye-spliced. The ends of the strands of the eye splice are used to worm down the cable. The whole eye and splice is marled and served with good rope and a thimble is seized in (Fig. 194).

To Make a Grommet.—Cut a strand about three and a half times the length of the grommet required. Unlay the rope carefully and keep the turns of the strand in. Close up the strand in the form of a ring (Fig. 195), and then pass the ends round and round in their original lay until all the intervals are filled up (Fig. 196), and then finish off the two ends as in a long splice (Fig. 197).

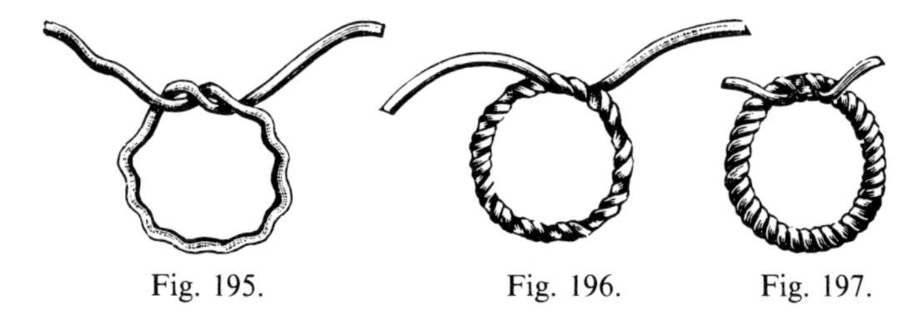

Fig. 195. Fig. 196. Fig. 197.

PURCHASES.

Note.—From the "power gained" in every case a deduction of 5 per cent. at least for each sheave must be made for friction losses.

Single Whip.—A rope rove through a single block fixed in any position. No power is gained (Fig. 198).

Fig. 198.

Double Whip.—A rope rove through two single blocks—upper block a tail block, lower one a movable hook block. Power gained—double (Fig. 199).

Fig. 199.

A Runner adds an additional power to the purchase it is used with. (Fig. 200).

Fig. 200.

Gun Tackle.—Two single blocks. Power gained—twice or thrice, according to which is the movable block (Fig. 201).

Fig. 201.

Handy Billy or Jigger.—A small tackle for general use; a double block with a tail and single block with hook (Fig. 202). Power gained—three or four times.

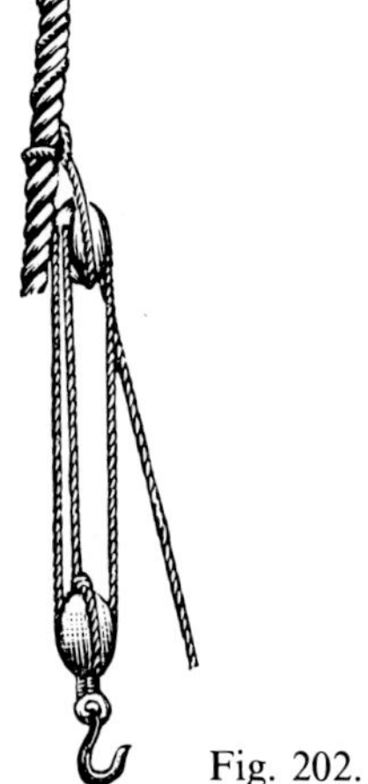

Fig. 202.

Watch Tackle or Luff Tackle.—Double hook block and single hook block (Fig. 203). Power gained—three or four times.

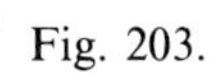

Fig. 203.

Double Luff.—Two double blocks (Fig. 204). Power gained—four or five times.

Fig. 204.

Three-fold Purchase.—Two three-fold blocks Power gained—six or seven times. (Fig. 205).

Fig. 205.

Four-fold Purchase.—Two four-fold blocks Power gained — eight or nine times. (Fig. 206).

NOTE.—When using multi-sheave blocks the tendency to twist may be reduced by arranging the rope so that it passes over the outer sheaves first and the hauling part comes from a centre sheave.

Fig. 206.

A Single Spanish Burton.—Two single blocks and a hook. Power gained—three times (Fig. 207).

Fig. 207.

A Double Spanish Burton.—There are two forms of this purchase—Fig. 208, by using three single blocks; Fig. 209, by using one double block and two single blocks. Power gained—five times.

Fig. 208.

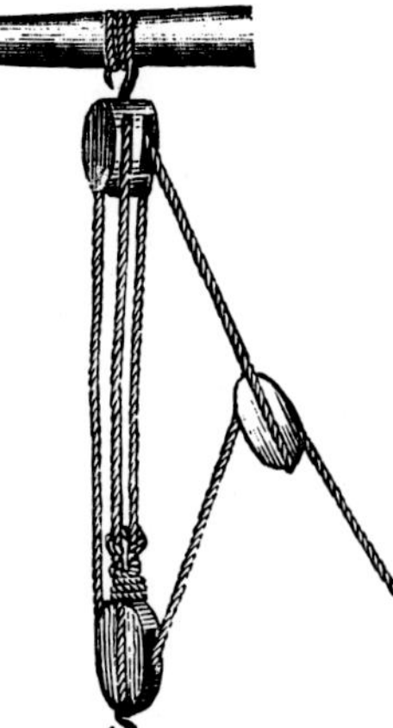

Fig. 209.

To Shorten a Sling.—Carry the lower end up the sling until the overall length is correct (Fig. 210). Grasp the sling at

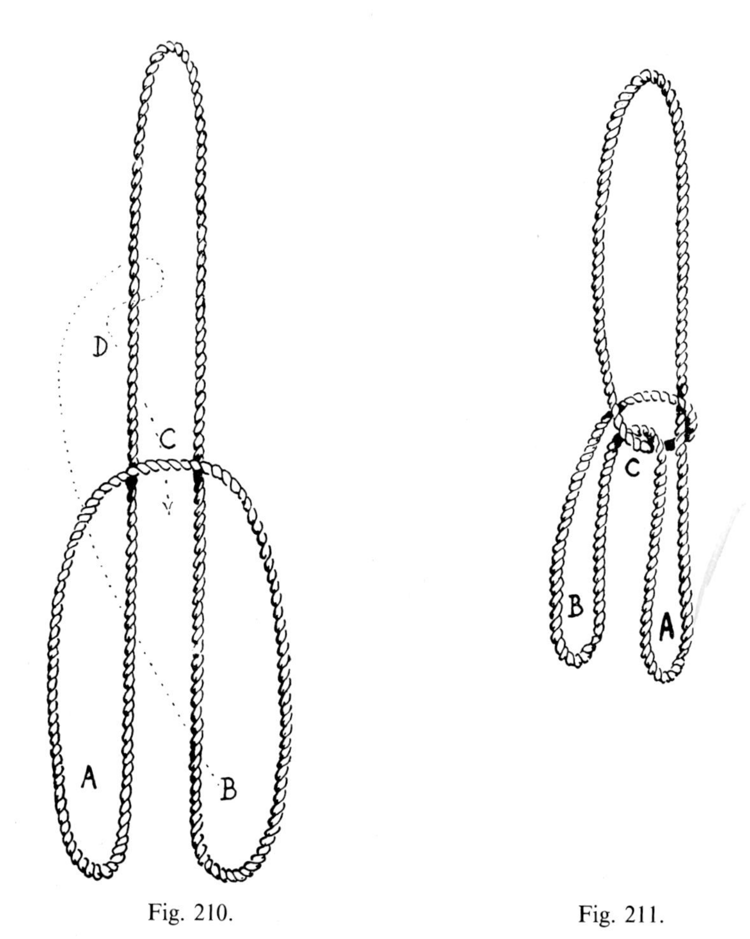

Fig. 210. Fig. 211.

the crossing *C*, and pass loop *B* around *D* and through the upper loop, above its own part (Fig. 211).

A Spanish Windlass.—To rig a Spanish Windlass take a good strand well greased in the centre. Place the strand over the two parts of the rope that are to be hove together, and bringing the ends of the strand under the bight and up again, place a bolt close to the strand. Take the ends of the strand and lay them up with their own parts so as to form two eyes. Take a round turn with these round the bolt, put a marline-spike through each eye and heave around (Fig. 212).

Fig. 212.

LASHINGS.

Three methods of lashing are commonly used when making structures by fastening spars together. Where two spars cross and have a tendency under load to slide over each other a "Square" lashing is used, although the spars may not actually be square with each other. Where the spars are used as bracings and under certain loads may tend to spring apart a "Diagonal" lashing is used. In the standard trestle (Fig. 213) all of the lashings are Square, except the centre one (D) which is Diagonal. Where two spars have to form legs and take a load between them a "Sheer" lashing is used (Fig. 214).

A variation of this is used when joining poles end to end (Fig. 215).

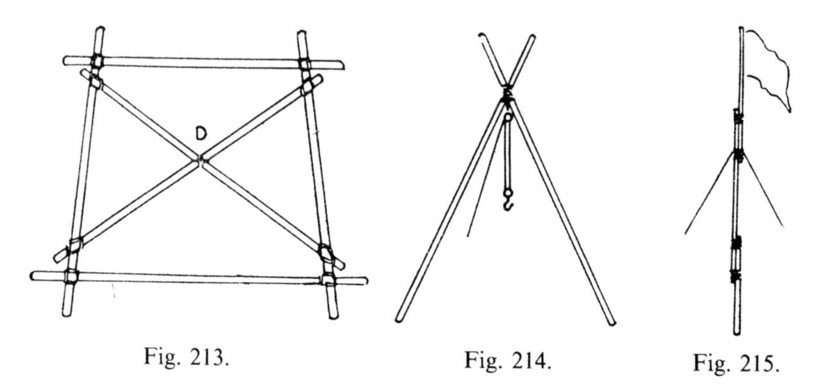

Fig. 213. Fig. 214. Fig. 215.

To make a Square lashing, put the spars in position and fasten the lashing to the one nearest vertical, below the other, with a clove hitch, and twist the end around the standing part (Fig. 216A). Take the lashing around the spars squarely (Fig. 216B) and follow round to make a total of three or four turns. To prevent the turns riding up, work on the inside of

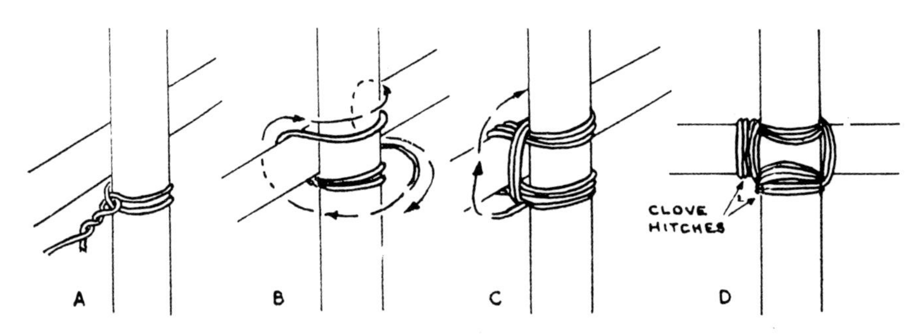

Fig. 216.

previous turns on one spar and the outside of them on the other spar. Pull all turns as tight as possible as they are made.

Further tightening is done by frapping turns, put on between the spars, pulled taut, and, if necessary, beaten into the main turns (Fig. 216C). After three or four frapping turns, finish with a clove hitch on the horizontal spar (Fig. 216D), arranging the crossing of the hitch where it will not slacken if the knot turns.

A Diagonal lashing is made after the ends of the spars have been square lashed. Put a timber hitch diagonally over the crossing (Fig. 217A) and draw it tight. Put on a total of three or four tight turns in the same direction, followed by three or four in the other directions (Fig. 217B). Make

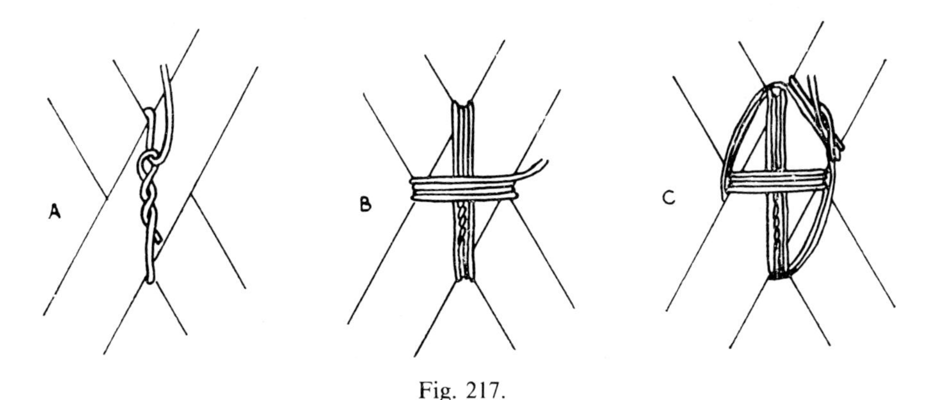

Fig. 217.

frapping turns between the spars and finish with a clove hitch on one of them (Fig. 217C).

A Sheer lashing is started on a pair of legs when they are

laid parallel. Put a clove hitch around one spar and twist the end around the standing part, then take turns around the two spars (Fig. 218A). The number of turns will depend on the sizes of rope and spars, and the purpose of the structure, but do not put on too many turns—ten would be enough for most purposes. Open the spars enough to admit frapping turns, without releasing the tension on the rope, then put on three or four frapping turns and finish with a clove hitch on the other spar at the other end of the lashing (Fig. 218B).

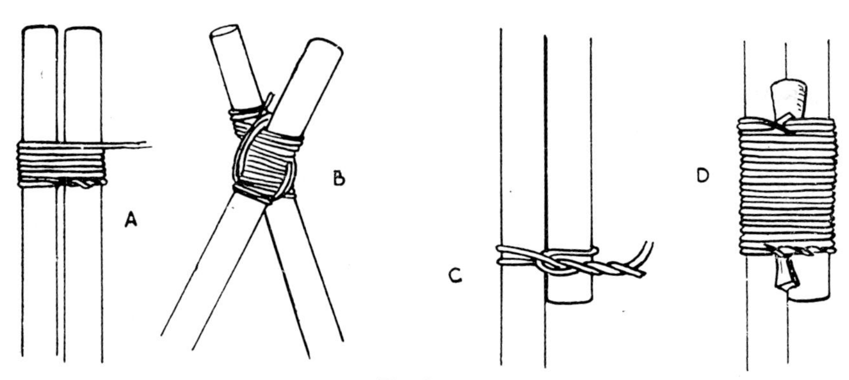

Fig. 218.

If the Sheer lashing is to be used to join poles end to end, allow sufficient overlap on the poles to admit two lashings. Start the lashing with a clove hitch around both poles (Fig. 218C). Put on the turns as tightly as possible and finish with a clove hitch around both poles. As frapping turns cannot be used, the lashing may be tightened by driving in wooden wedges (Fig. 218D).

MISCELLANEOUS.

A Flat Seizing.—This is only a light seizing and it is used when no great strain will be put on it. For clearness, the two ropes that are to be seized together are called Shrouds and the rope worked round them is called the Seizing.

Splice an eye in one end of the seizing. Take it round both of the shrouds, through its own eye, and heave taut.

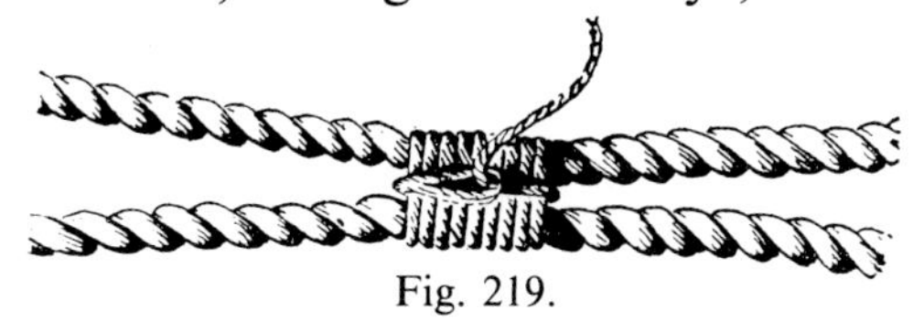

Fig. 219.

Take as many turns as required round both shrouds, heaving them taut. Then pass the end of the seizing down below the turns and in the space left by the rounds of the shrouds, and bring it out through the eye of the seizing.

Then take a round turn with the seizing passing between the shrouds and over the turns already made, and heave taut with a heaver. Then pass the seizing round again twice forming a clove-hitch, one part of which lies on each side of round turn first made. These turns are called Frapping Turns (Fig. 219).

A Round Seizing.—This seizing is used where the strain on both "shrouds" is the same, and where the flat seizing would not be strong enough.

Begin as for a flat seizing and pass the requisite number of turns, say seven. Reeve the seizing back under the turns and out through the eye. The first layer of turns is called the

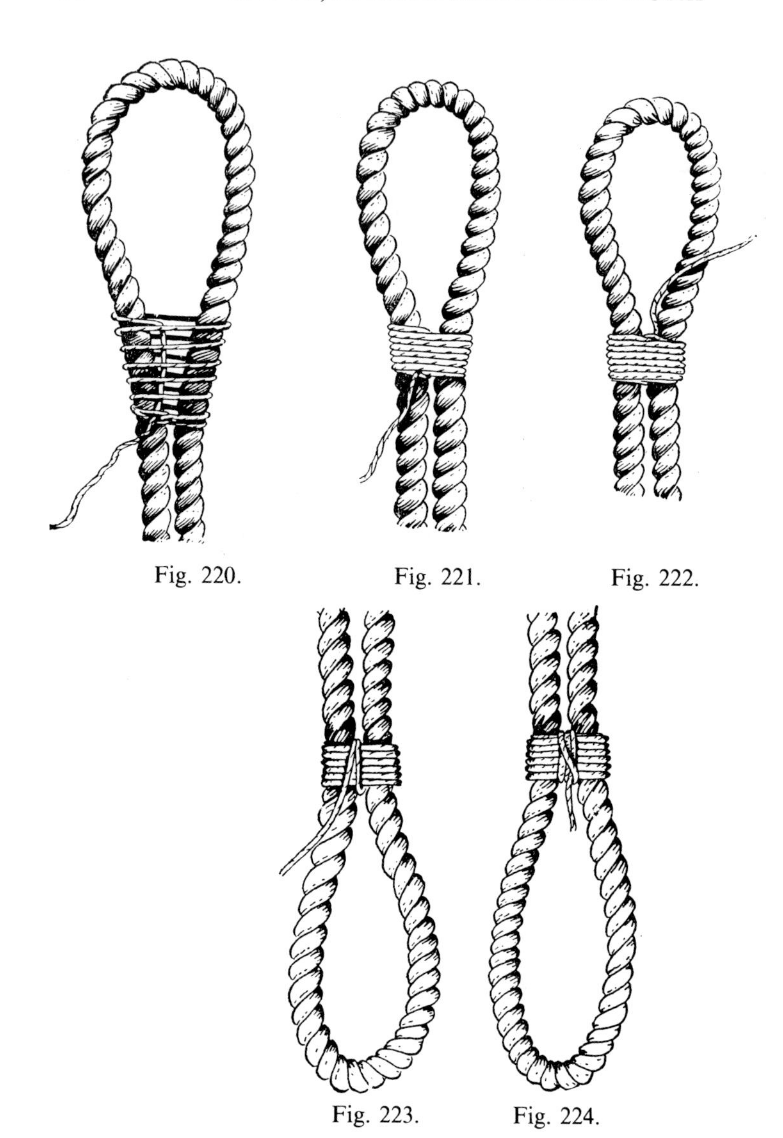

Fig. 220. Fig. 221. Fig. 222.

Fig. 223. Fig. 224.

the lower turns and these should be hove taut with a heaver (Fig. 220).

The upper turns are now put on and they lie in the hollow between the turns of the lower turns.

When the sixth turn has been put on, the end of the seizing is tucked below the last turn of the lower turns and hove taut (Fig. 221). Then finish as for the flat seizing by putting on the frapping turns (Figs. 223 and 224).

A Throat Seizing.—A Throat Seizing was used for turning in deadeyes, hearts, blocks, etc.

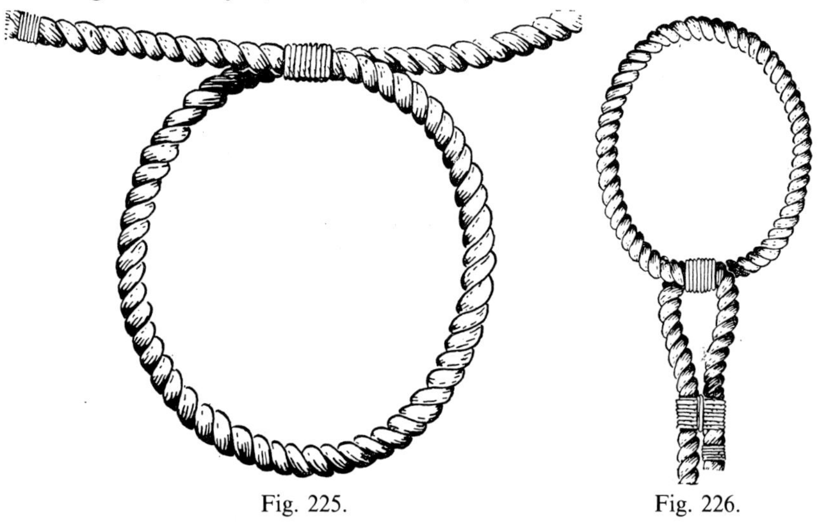

Fig. 225. Fig. 226.

The rope is turned in to a bight and a round seizing is put on, but without frapping turns (Fig. 225).

The end of the rope is then turned up and secured to the standing part by a Round Seizing (Fig. 226).

A Racking Seizing.—This seizing is used when an unequal strain is put on the two "shrouds", as, for instance, when a deadeye is turned in.

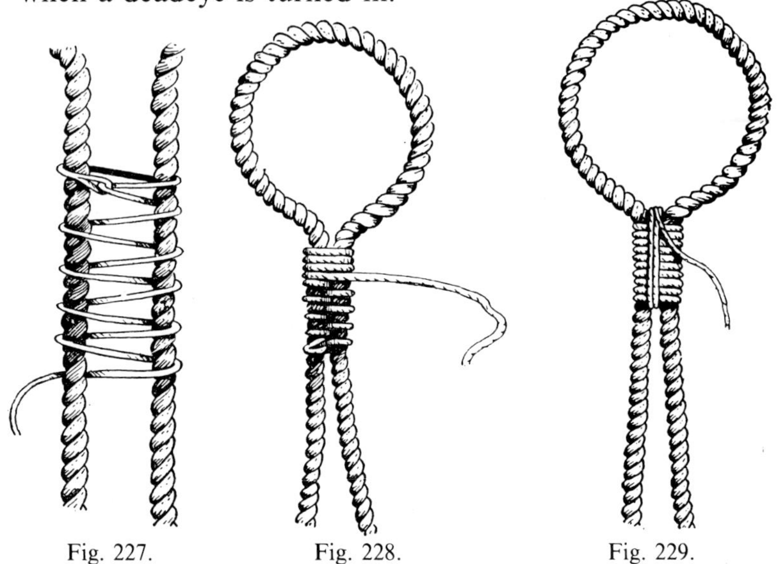

Fig. 227. Fig. 228. Fig. 229.

The seizing is begun in the same way as for a flat or a round seizing. The seizing rope is then dipped between the two shrouds and the turns are made in the form of racking turns as shewn in the figure but closer together, leaving just space enough between them for the round turns to lie. The usual number of racking turns is 13 (Fig. 227).

The end of the seizing is dipped inside the last turn and the roundabout turns are made, working back towards the eye at the beginning of the seizing. These roundabout turns lie in the spaces between the racking turns (Fig. 228).

When the last roundabout turn is passed the seizing is finished in the same way as the flat and the round seizings (Fig. 229).

The seizing rope itself is usually finished of by having a Crown and a Wall Knot worked on it.

An Artificial or Spindle Eye.—This is a useful form of "eye" on braided ropes but can also be made on laid ropes.

Unlay the end of the rope, open the strands and separate each yarn.

Take a piece of wood (the spindle) whose diameter is slightly larger than the inside diameter of the desired eye. The slight increase of diameter is to allow for the service and cockscombing. On the spindle raise two lumps with marline or spunyarn. These lumps should be about as high as half the diameter of the rope on which the eye is to be formed, and their top edges should be distant from one another about the diameter of the rope. These are shewn at *a b* on Fig. 230.

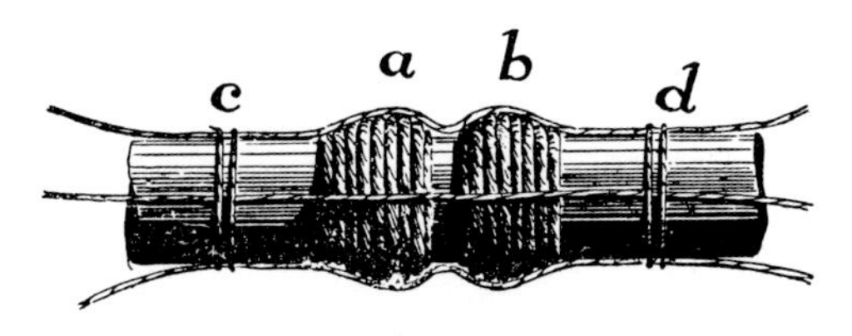

Fig. 230.

Now lay four pieces of seaming twine along the spindle at intervals round it, and stopper them in place as shewn at *c d* (Fig. 230).

Now take the rope and hitch the strands in pairs round the spindle in the space between the lumps *a b* as shewn in Fig. 231. These lumps were made to prevent the strands from spreading out on the spindle. Continue hitching the strands until they have all been used and be careful not to bring all the hitches at the same place as that would cause a bulge.

Lay all the ends of the strands down alongside the rope and pass a few turns of seaming twine round them.

Cut the stoppers at *c* and *d*, bring the ends of the pieces of seaming twine up and knot them tightly round the hitched strands. These ties will keep the eye in good shape.

One of the lumps *a* or *b* can now be taken off and the eye slid off the spindle.

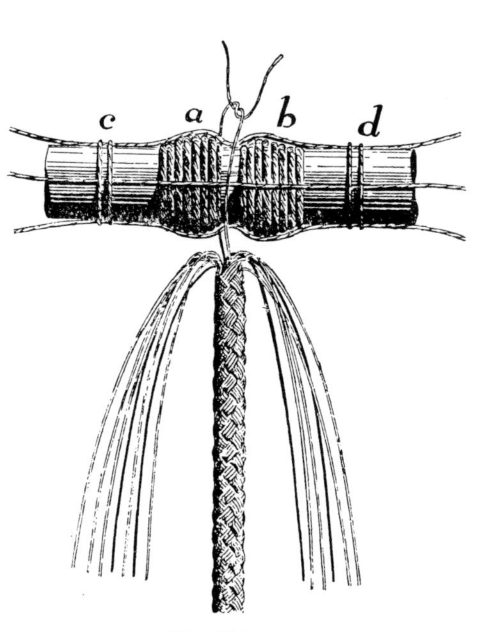

Fig. 231.

Commencing at the top, the eye should now be tightly served down to the fork on both sides. Then the tails of the strands are scraped down taper and served down. Finally, the eye may be finished off with cockscombing.

To Point a Rope End.—First put a stop on at three times the circumference of the rope from the end, which will leave about the length for pointing, unlay the rope to the stop and then unlay the strands. Split the number of the outside yarns and make a nettle out of each yarn. (A nettle is made by laying up the yarns with the finger and thumb left-handed). When an even number of nettles has been made

Fig. 232.

stop them back on the standing part of the rope. Then form a heart with the rest of the yarns by scraping them down to a proper size with a knife, and marl them down together with twine very tightly; divide the nettles, taking every other one up and every other one down. Pass three turns with a piece of twine—which is called the warp—very taut round the part where the nettles separate, taking a hitch with the last turn. Continue to repeat this process by placing every alternate nettle up and down, passing the warp or "filling", taking a hitch each time, until the point is to its required length. It is generally finished off by working a small eye in the end (Figs. 232 and 233).

Another form of finish for a rope "point" is shewn in Fig. 234. It is used on ropes of ordinary size. Fig. 233 is more suitable for very large ropes. Fig. 234 shews a "Point" where the heart is not scraped down almost to a point. The finish is made by keeping one set of nettles *a a a* down along the heart, then the other set of nettles *b b b* are hitched round the warp, leaving an eye on each of them. The second and the hitching turns are then threaded through these eyes and hauled tight. The nettles, *b b b*, are then hauled tight and everything trimmed off.

Fig. 233.

Fig. 234.

A very pleasing variety of point can be made as follows:—

Make nettles as required but in multiples of three. Then when working leave two of each three down and take one up. After the warp is passed and hitched turn down one and take up one of each set and again pass the warp. This always leaves two down and one up. When the point is finished it will be found to have a spiral effect.

A still better spiral effect can be got by making nettles in multiples of four. Leave three down and take one up. After the warp is passed and hitched turn down one of each set and pass the warp again. This always leaves three down and one up.

A zig-zag pattern may be made in a similar way. After doing a number of rounds as above, taking up the nettle to right of the one which is turned down, do a similar number of rounds but take up the nettle to the left of the one which is turned down.

Another very good finish for a point is the Ron finish. This consists of a Footrope Knot worked over the end of the heart. When used to finish a point or cross point, after the work on the nettles and warp has reached almost the desired length, lay back four or six nettles equally spaced round the work. With these nettles form a Footrope Knot over the remaining nettles. Trim off the heart with a rounded end and cut off the ends of the nettles not used for the Footrope

A. *B.* *C.*

THREE ROPE "POINTS".

A. This has a Footrope Knot of eight parts, followed round twice. The "pointing" of half-hitching and the finish is a Footrope Knot in four parts, crowned and followed round.

B. The "pointing" is of coach whipping finished with a Footrope Knot crowned. A five part Turk's Head is at the bottom of the pointing.

C. This pointing is worked spiral in multiples of three, two down and one up, as described after Fig. 164. The top is a Diamond Knot of five nettles, crowned and followed round. A five parts Turk's Head is at the bottom.

Knot. Then crown the Footrope Knot over the rounded end of the heart and follow round the strands in the usual way.

Half Hitching.—This is a very effective way of covering a rope point, a rope, a ball or a bottle. A palm and needle are required and the process is often called "Palm and Needle Hitching".

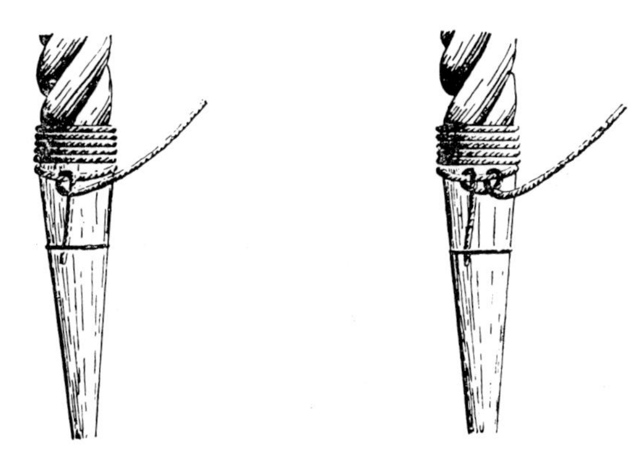

Fig. 235. Fig. 236.

The process is very simple and consists in putting on series of half hitches as shewn in Figs. 235 and 236. On a rope point a very good way is to begin by putting on a Footrope Knot over the seizing. Then make the first row of hitches through the outer turn of the Footrope Knot. Each row is then hitched through the bights of the preceding row. To finish off, make another Footrope Knot at the end of the "point" as already described and pass the last row of hitches through the lowest turn of the knot.

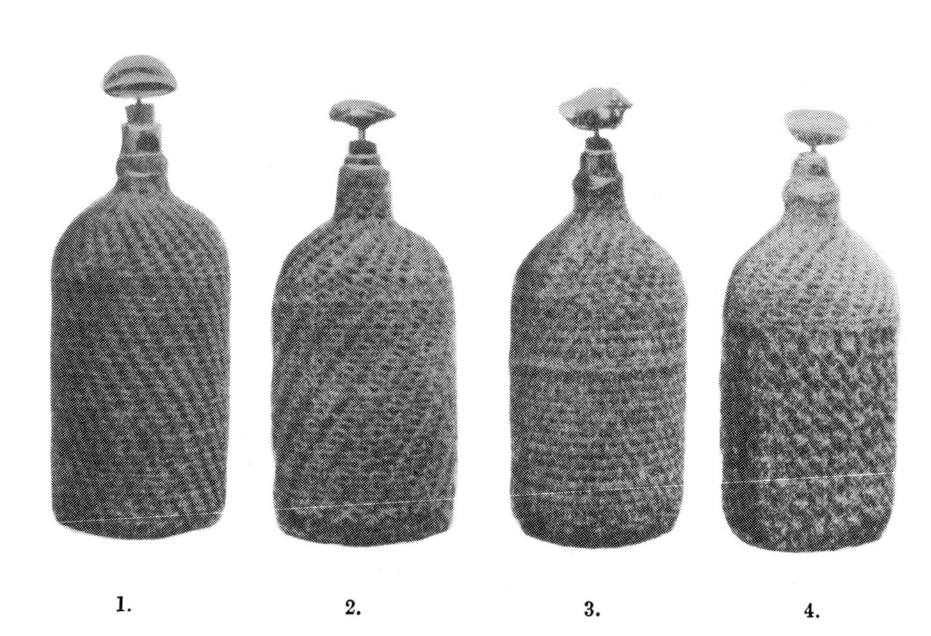

1. 2. 3. 4.

FOUR BOTTLES COVERED WITH KNOT WORK.

No. 1. This is half-hitching.

No. 2. This is half-hitching, the hitches being alternately made overhand and underhand.

No. 3. This is covered with pointing.

No. 4. This is covered with interlaced netting.

The shoulders, necks and bottoms are covered with half hitching.

Note, when inserting the strands of which the Footrope Knot is to be made a good way is to put them through the heart of the point about half an inch from the end. Then carry the half hitching over these strands until almost at the end of the heart. Then form the Footrope Knot, and pass the last row of half hitches through the lowest turn. In this way the Footrope Knot is securely anchored to the heart.

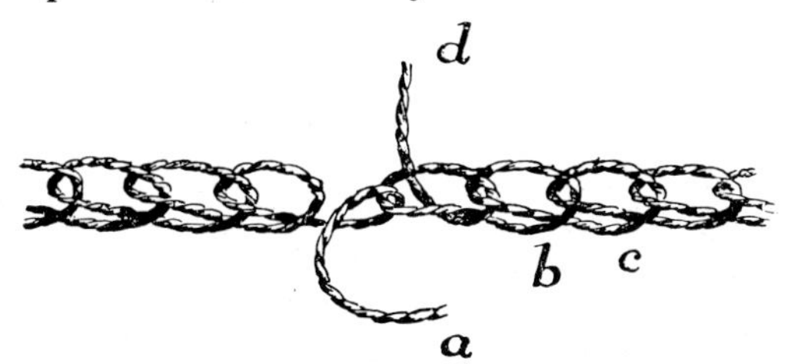

Fig. 237.

When it is desired to cover with half hitching a bottle or other hard object, a good way is to commence by making a length of chain plait sufficient to reach round the largest part and hitch the ends together as shewn in Fig. 237. Keeping the loose end *a* tight, the working end *d* is hitched through loops to the left. Another good way to commence is to cast on round the object a Turk's Head with as many tucks or turns as possible. The hitching is then done through the loops of the Turk's Head. When the hitches begin to come too close together owing to the taper of the bottle, miss a loop at intervals. Several variations can be made in the pattern, by reversing the hitches for instance.

The commonest use for half hitching is to cover fenders, etc.

Pineapple Knot.—This could be used to cover a "mouse" on a stay, a raised handle on a rope, etc.

Begin by raising a "mouse" of the required size on the rope. This is done by winding on marline or yarns.

With a pricker, stick two pieces of cord through the "mouse" near one end and at right angles to another. These chords must be long enough to make the knot.

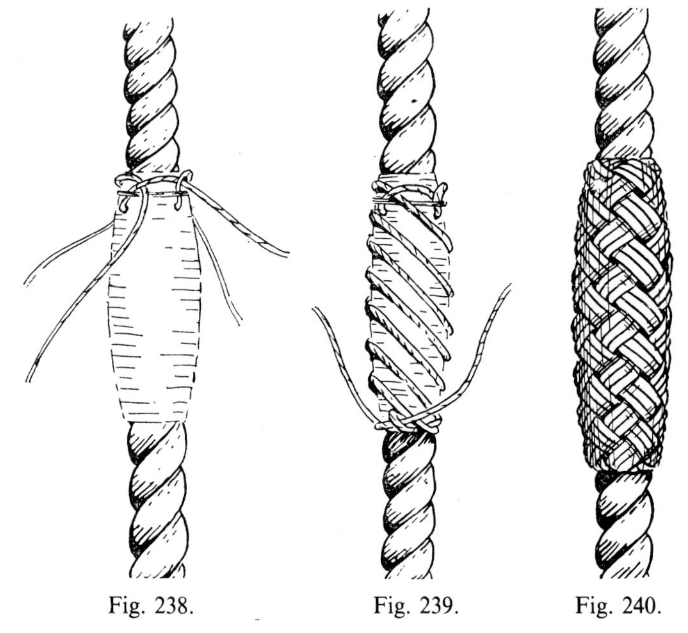

Fig. 238. Fig. 239. Fig. 240.

Put a whipping on them and crown them as shewn in Fig. 238. Take the chords down spirally round the "mouse" and secure them by a temporary whipping. Then crown them upwards left handed as shewn in Fig. 239.

The chords are then worked back to the top end, tucking them against the spiral over one and under one. This locks everything and the temporary whipping can be cut off.

Then follow round until the "mouse" is covered closely with what is cross-pointing (Fig. 240).

If desired, three or more chords can be used.

Pineapple Knot. (Another method.)—The figures shew this knot made with four strands but it may be made with any number of strands. The knot may be made as a Fancy Knot on the end of a rope or it may be on a lead line to mark the 50 fathoms and 100 fathoms. In this case the strands are got by sticking pieces of line through the log line.

The knot may be made of any length.

Put a seizing round the strands, and at a distance about equal to the desired length of the Pineapple Knot, crown the strands as shewn in Fig. 241. This is the first stage.

Then lead each strand over the one to its right and under the next as in Fig. 242—Second stage.

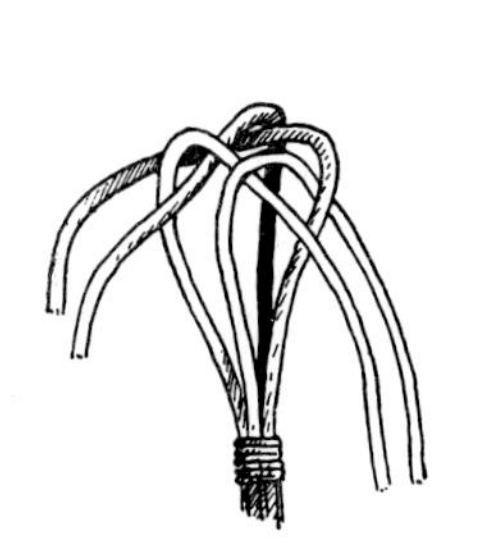

Fig. 241.—First Stage.

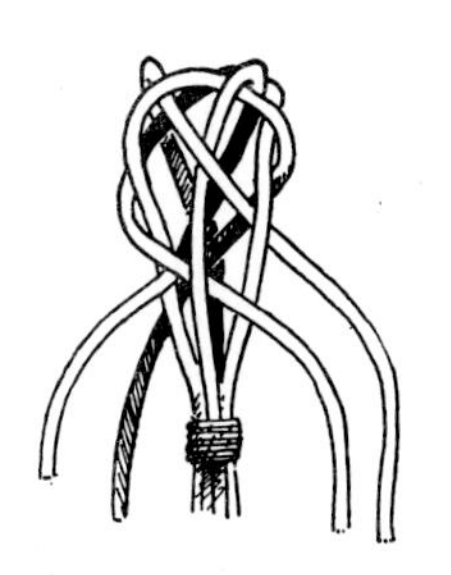

Fig. 242.—Second Stage.

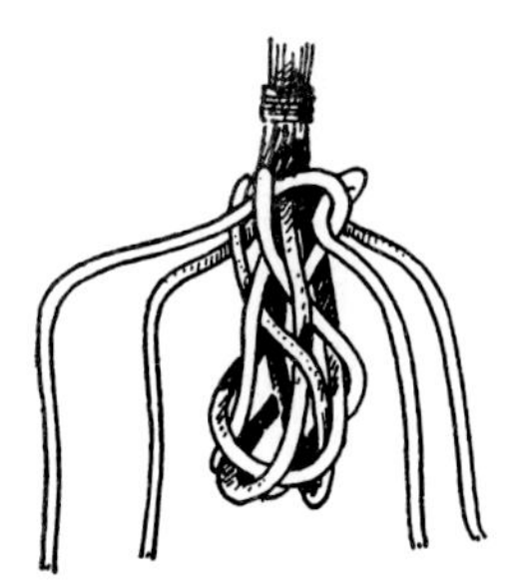

Fig. 243.—Third Stage.

Reverse the knot and crown the strands as shewn in sketch. (Fig. 243—Third stage).

Fig. 244.—Fourth Stage. Fig. 245.—Fifth Stage.

Follow round each strand till they all come out at the bottom of the knot again as shewn in sketch. (Fig. 244—Fourth stage).

The knot may be followed round again as desired and the ends tucked up through the centre of the knot and cut off or opened out into a tassle. (Fig. 245—Fifth stage).

The knot may be made, if desired, over a heart or core.

Spanish Hitching.—This is a method of covering rope, etc., which is very simple. It is made with a number of hitching strands *a a* and one filling or warping strand *b*, as shewn in Figs. 246 and 247.

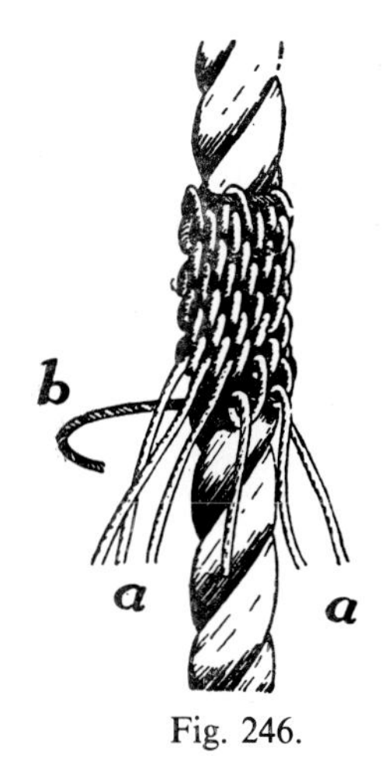

Fig. 246.

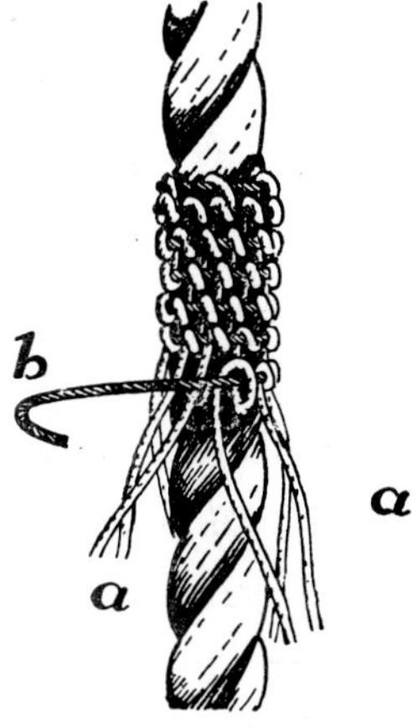

Fig. 247.

With the warping strand "middle" the requisite number of hitching strands round the rope. Then put a hitch round the warping strand with each of the hitching strands in succession, taking care to keep the warping strand tight.

Two patterns are shewn in Figs. 246 and 247. In one of them the hitches are made "outside" turn and on the other "inside" turn.

Coach Whipping or Cross Pointing.—This is essentially the same as round sennit, but instead of being used to make a braided line (sennit) it is used to cover such things as a stanchion, a telescope or a rope point.

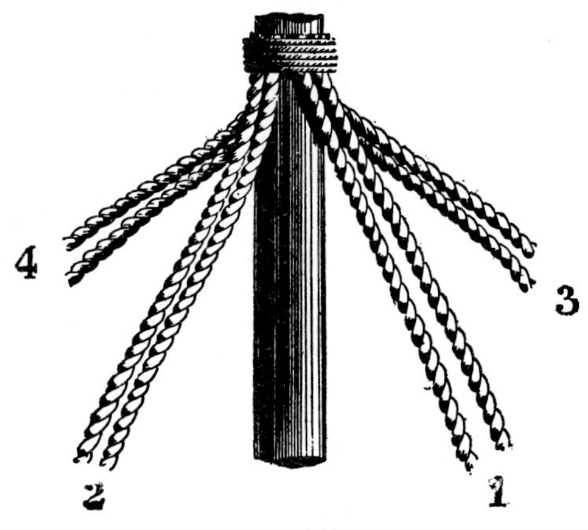

Fig. 248.

It can be made with any even number of strands and these strands are often laid double, or treble. The Figs. 248, 249, 250 and 251 shew the strands laid double.

As a rule, coach whipping is a "two man job", one to do the laying and the other to hold the laid up strands, but it can be done by one man if using only four strands.

Having stoppered on to the stanchion the four strands as shewn in Fig. 248, take strand 1 and lay it across to the left and strand 2 and lay it across to the right as in Fig. 249.

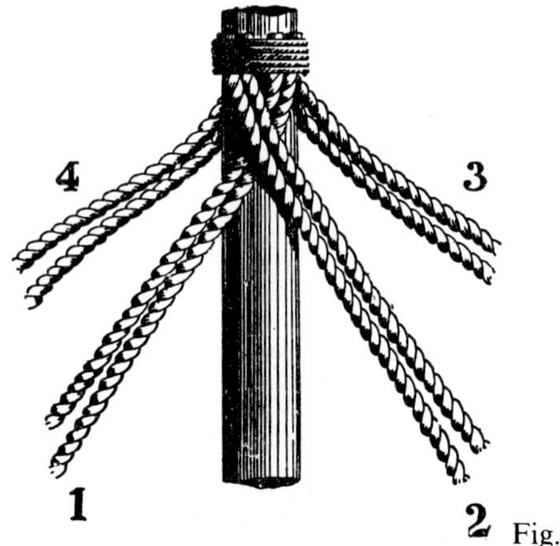

Fig. 249.

Then take strand 4 under the stanchion below 3 and lead it back over 2 to its own side (left). Then take strand 3 under

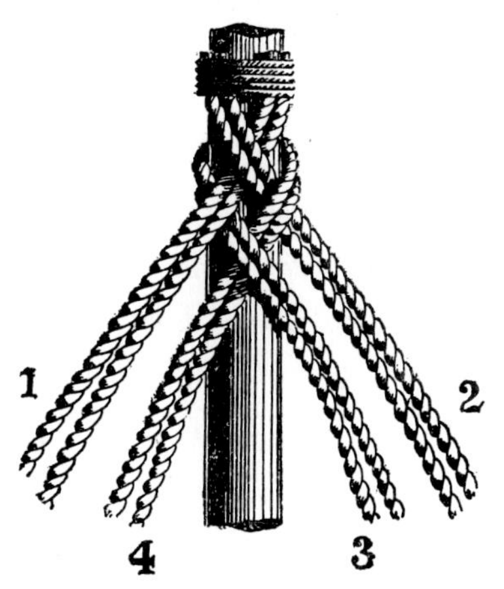

Fig. 250.

the stanchion below 1, over 4 and back to its own side (right) as shewn in Fig. 250.

The work now proceeds by taking strand 1 under the stanchion below 2, over 3 and back to its own side (left) and so on working from one side and then the other and using the topmast strand. Fig. 251 shews the work.

Fig. 251.

When a very close whipping is desired it is a good way to work, say, double strands and then work in a single strand alongside each to make treble strands.

When more than four strands are required, as already mentioned, it is a two man job.

Seize the requisite even number of strands round the object to be covered. Then the "boatswain" divides them and passes each alternate strand to his "mate", laying the other strands down towards himself. He then takes a strand from the "mate" and lays it down over his corresponding strand on its right and passes that strand to the "mate" in exchange for the strand he has taken from him. He goes on all round in this way till he has taken all the strands originally held by the "mate" and given the "mate" all the strands originally held by himself. Then he takes a strand from the "mate" and lays it down over its corresponding strand on its left and passes that strand to the "mate" in exchange and so on to complete the round, working right and left in alternate rounds.

In this way it will be found that one set of strands works round to the right and the other set to the left.

The Figs. 257 to 263 illustrating round sennit shew the process.

SENNITS.

Sennits are braided ropes of various kinds.

Common sennit is made with any odd number of strands. The simplest form is three ply (Fig. 252). The figs. 253 and 254 shew seven ply sennit but the method of working is the same.

Fig. 252.

The ends of the strands having been secured, divide them so that there is one more on one side than on the other. Take the outer strand from the lot having the greater number and bring it over to the middle and add it to the opposite lot of strands, thus giving it a majority. Then take the outside strand from that side, bring it across to the middle and add it to the other lot. Fig. 253 shews the strands so treated, but the strands have been brought too far and across. Fig. 254 shews the process much better.

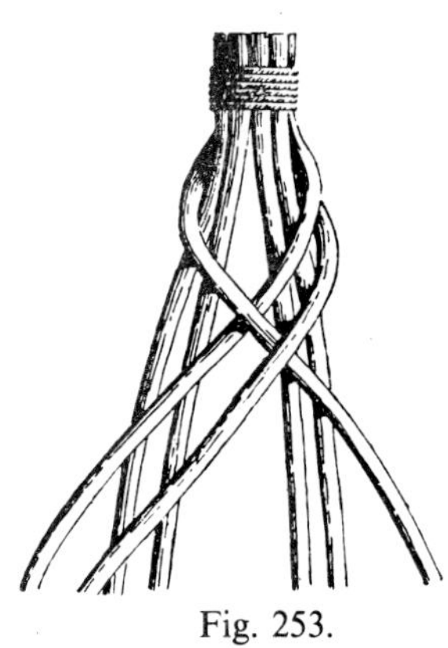

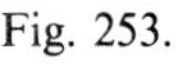

Fig. 253.

Fig. 254.

English or Flat Sennit.—This can be made with any number of strands. Secure them over a line or rod. Take the right hand strand and, passing it alternately under and over the other strands, bring it out on the left. Take the next strand on the right and repeat the process and so on, as shewn in Fig. 255. For clearness the figure had been drawn very "open". In practice the strands would be pulled up tightly, and if the sennit is very wide the strands as they are brought across would be pushed home with a flat piece of wood.

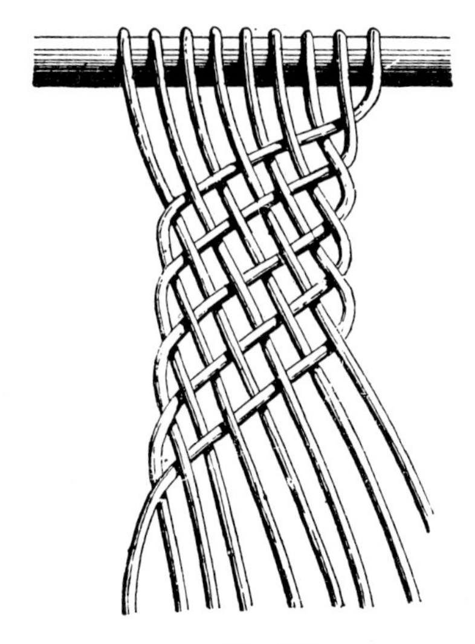

Fig. 255.

French Sennit.—This is made with an uneven number of strands and is worked from both sides towards the centre. Divide the strands so that there is an extra one on one side. Take the outside strand of the larger lot, the right hand lot (Fig. 256), and work it under and over he strands of its own lot to the centre, bring it across the centre and add it to the inside of the left-hand lot. The left hand lot has now four strands. Take the outside left hand strand, work it under and over the strands to the centre and add it to the inside of the right hand lot. The work then proceeds, taking the outside strands from each side alternately, working them under and over to the centre and adding them to the opposite lot.

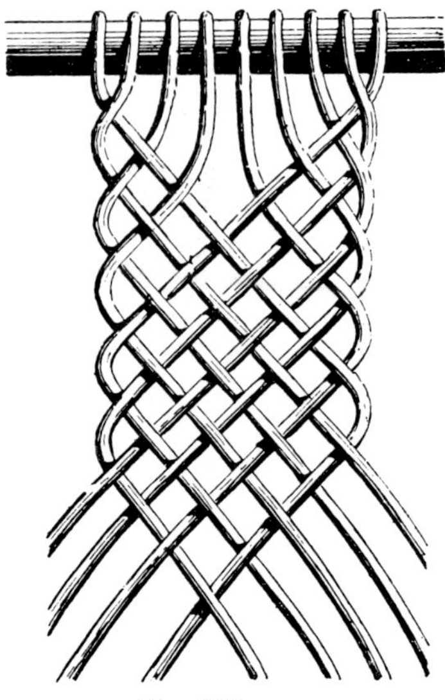

Fig. 256.

Round Senit.—Round sennit or braided rope may be made with four, six or any even number of strands. If made with more than four strands it will look better if it be made round a heart or core. The illustrations do not shew this heart.

The Figs. 257, 258, 259, 260 and 261, 262 and 263 shew round sennit of six strands.

Begin by crossing each pair of neighbouring strands as in Fig. 257, holding one of each down and allowing the other to stand up. It will be found that one set is going round to the left (in this case the plain strands) and the other set to the right.

Fig. 257.

Take one of the upright strands, *a*, and following round the way it is going (to the right) pass it over the plain strand on its right, and, holding the strand *a* down pull the plain strand upright. When the three upright, shaded strands *a, b, c* have been so treated, Fig. 258 shews the result.

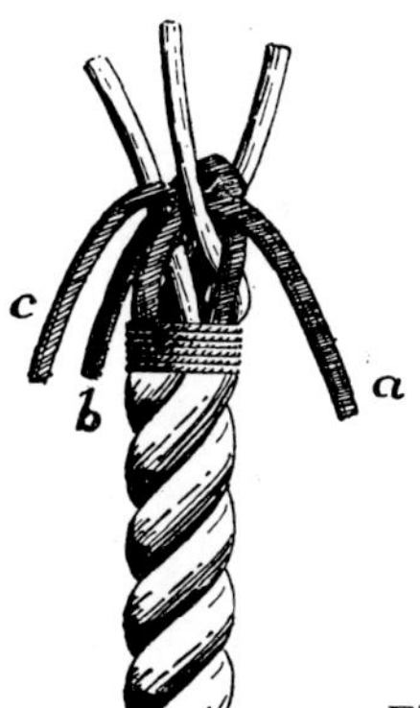

Fig. 258.

The same process is now carried out with the upright plain strands but towards the left, the plain strands being taken down to the left over the shaded strands, which are brought up (Figs. 259 and 260).

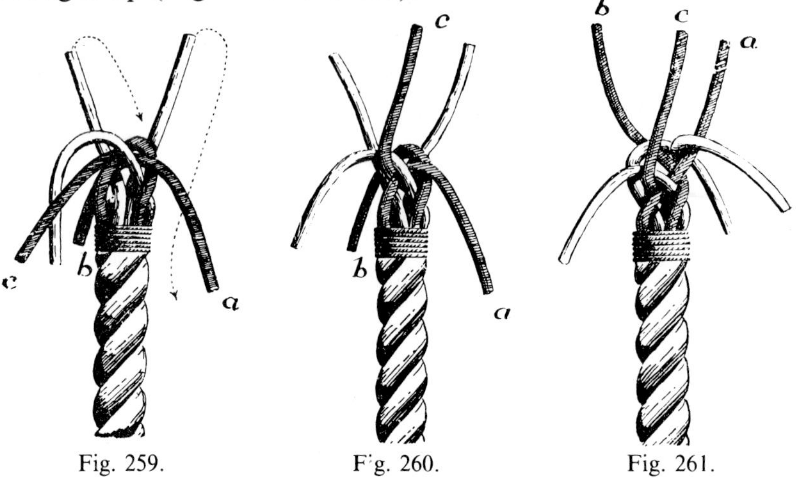

Fig. 259. Fig. 260. Fig. 261.

Figs. 261, 262 and 263 shew the process completed.

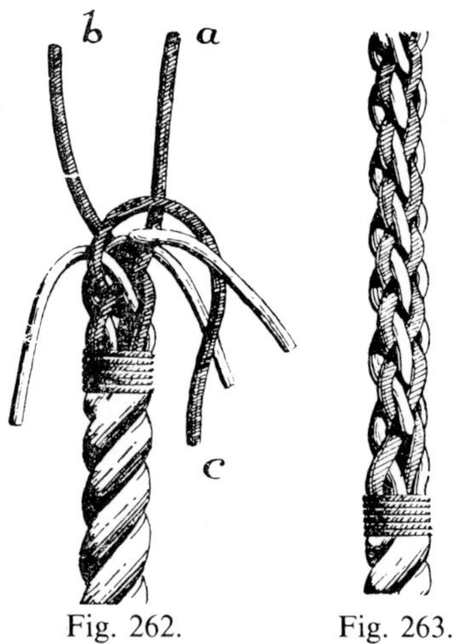

Fig. 262. Fig. 263.

The description makes the job seem complicated. In reality it is very simple.

Square Sennit.—This can be made of 8, 12 or 16 strands. Besides being made for fancy work it is used to make square section engine packing.

Square Sennit of Eight Strands.—Divide the strands into two lots of four each (Fig. 264). Then take one strand

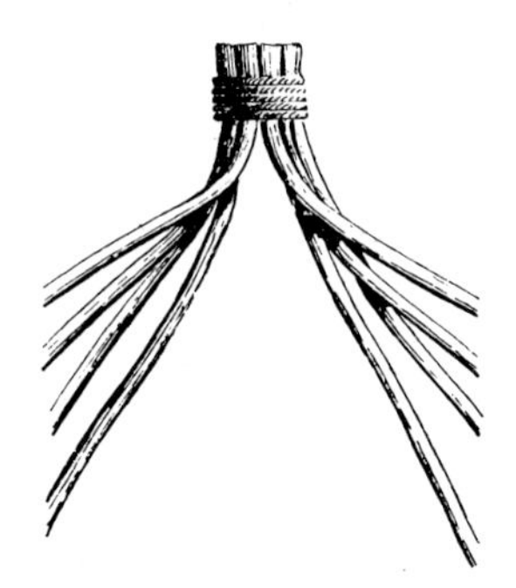

Fig. 264.

from the right hand lot, lead it round the back and up, leading it inside two strands of the left hand lot, and bring it back to its own, the right hand, lot. This is shewn in Fig. 265.

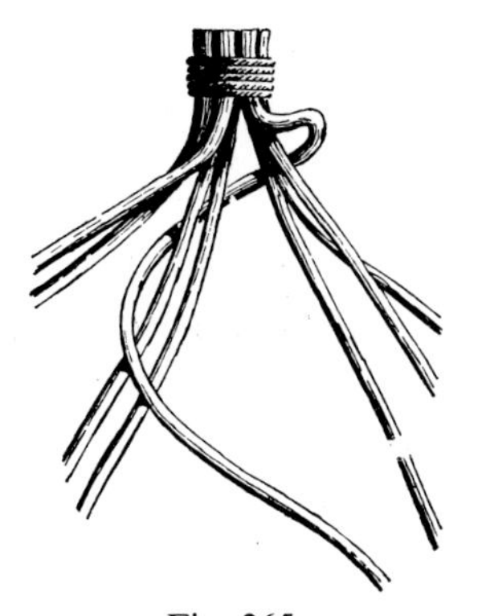

Fig. 265.

This leaves us with four strands in each lot. Now take a strand from the left hand lot, lead it round the back and inside two strands of the right hand lot and back to its own, left hand, lot. Proceed in this way taking a strand alternately from the right and the left and square sennit is the result. The first two or three passes are irregular but the sennit soon assumes the proper shape.

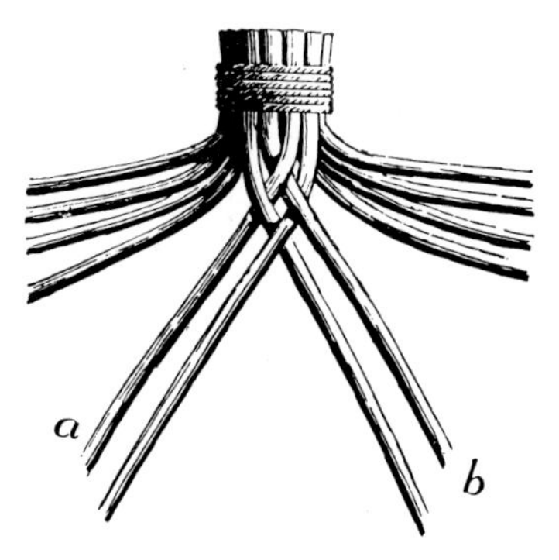

Fig. 266.

Square Sennit of Twelve or of Sixteen Strands.—In making square sennit of 12 strands, begin by plaiting the four centre strands and keeping four strands out on each side as shewn in Fig. 266. This will give six strands on each side. Then take the outside strand on the right hand side, pass it round the back and up through the middle of the left hand lot of strands, and bring it back to its own lot over three of the left hand lot of strands. This leaves six strands in each lot (Fig. 267).

Now take the top strand of the left hand lot. Pass it round the back and up through the middle of the right hand

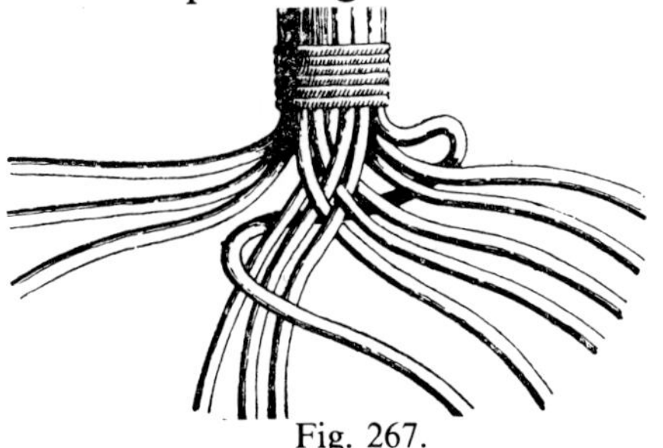

Fig. 267.

lot of strands, and bring it back to its own lot over three of the right hand lot of strands. By continuing this process, alternately right and left, a square sennit is made (Fig. 268).

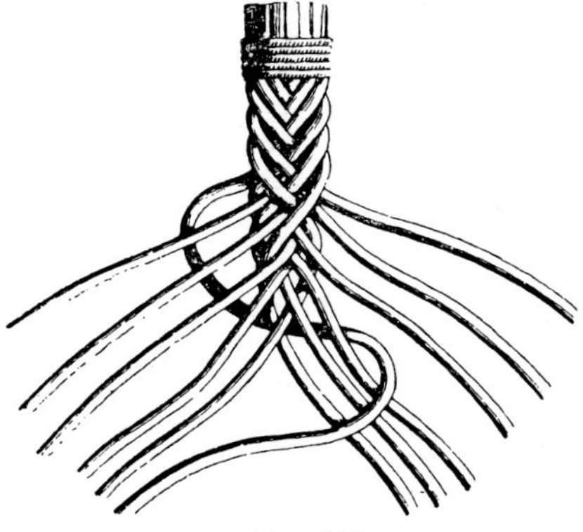

Fig. 268.

The process for 16 strand sennit is similar, only the outside strand is round the back and up through the middle of the opposite hand strands, *i.e.* over 4 and back to its own side.

Fig. 269.

When making Square Sennit it is best to work with each hand alternately. Bring down the strand from the left rear with the right hand, passing it through those strands where it will have to go. After you pass one of these over and in front of the two at the centre, nip all three with the finger and thumb of the right hand. Then do the same with the left hand, bringing down the top strand from the right rear, nip it with the left finger and thumb and let go with the right, leaving that hand free for the next stage. You can work quickly and certainly in this way.

The same procedure applies to Half-round Sennit.

Half-round Sennit is made in the same way as square sennit of eight strands but with six strands only. That is to say, the six strands are divided into two lots of three each. One outside strand on the right is led round the back and up inside two strands and over one strand of the left hand lot and back to its own side. This being repeated alternately from right and left produces a half round sennit (Fig. 269).

Half-round Sennit (another pattern).—Half-round, or at least sennit with a flat side, can also be made with eight parts.

This is made as shewn in Figs. 266 and 267, Square Sennit, but each strand is laid round the back and up inside one strand only instead of inside two strands, and back to its own side.

Portuguese Sennit or Boatswain's Plait.—This can be made flat or spiral. It is made by two strands worked around a heart consisting of one or two straight strands.

Fig. 270 shews the "Flat Portuguese Sennit". Middle the working part through the heart at *x* (or use two strands of a rope and leave the third as a heart). Lead one strand *a* under the heart *c*. Lead the other strand *b* under *a*, over *c* and through the bight of *a*. Haul tight. Repeat, but work *b* under *c* and *a* under *b* over *c* and through the bight of *b*. Continue this process using each strand alternately.

Fig. 271 shews "Spiral Portuguese Sennit".

This is made in the same way as flat Portuguese sennit except that, instead of working alternately from one side and then the other, work always from one side.

A similar Plait may be used to cover a rope or other article. It is made with any convenient number of strands arranged round the rope. The covering is made by making

Wall Knots with the strands alternately right hand and left hand. Crown Knots (which are just Wall Knots made upside down) may be used in the same way.

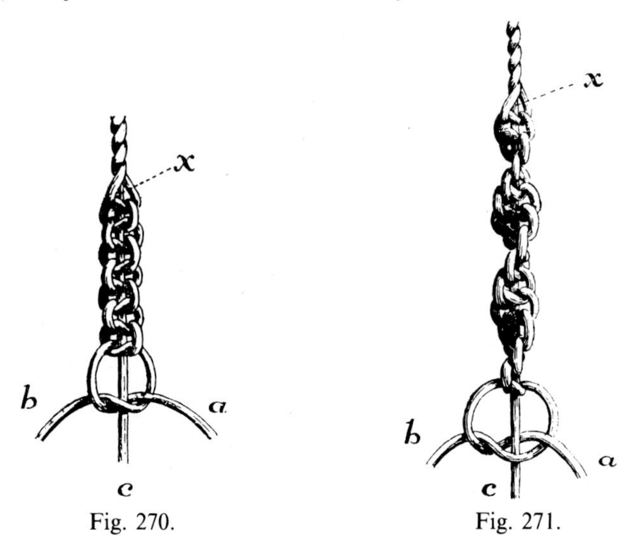

Fig. 270. Fig. 271.

Double Carrick Single Sennit.—This is better laid out on a board with pins. For clearness it is drawn open. It should be followed round twice. Fig. 272.

Fig. 272.

Overhand Knot Plaits.—These plaits may be made with 4, 6 or 8 strands.

Four Strand.—An Overhand Knot is made with two opposite strands, them an Overhand Knot is made with the other two strands, This process continued makes the plait. (Fig. 273).

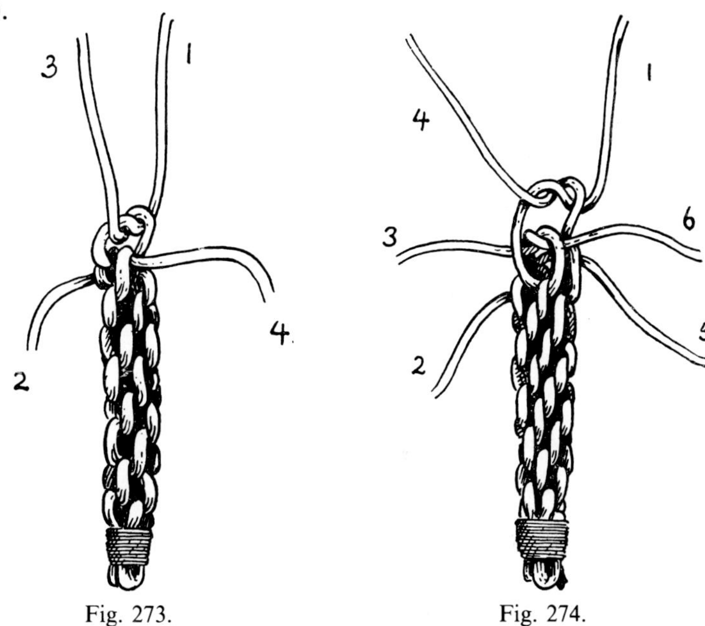

Fig. 273. Fig. 274.

Six Strand.—An Overhand Knot is made with two opposite strands—1 and 4—then an Overhand Knot is made with the two adjacent strands—2 and 5—and then with strands 3 and 6. This process is then repeated (Fig. 274).

Eight Strand.—An Overhand Knot is made with strands 1 and 4, and an Overhand Knot with strands 5 and 8. These

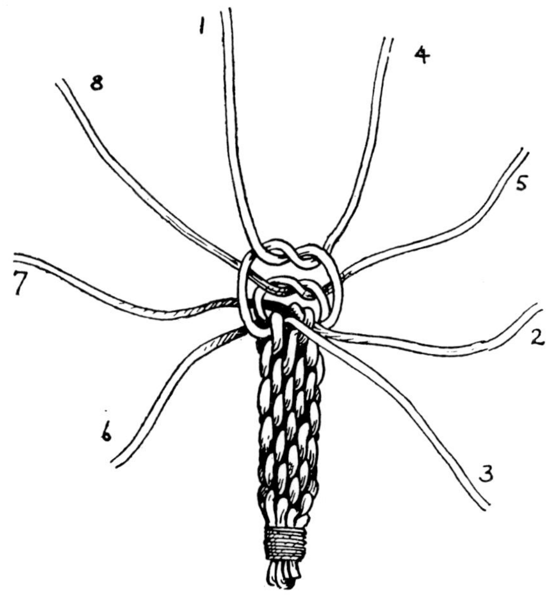

Fig. 275.

knots lie parallel across the plait. Then Overhand Knots are made with strands 2 and 7 and 3 and 6, and the process is then repeated (Fig. 275).

Turk's Head.—The Turk's Head is probably used more frequently in Fancy Work than any other knot. It may be varied in several ways. The number of turns may be varied. That is to say, the number of times that the chord of which the knot is made reaches the end of the knot and turns back may be varied.

The number of parts may be varied. If a line be drawn from one end of the knot to the other it will "cut" the chord in a number of places. The number of these "cuts" is the number of parts in the knot, and the length of the knot depends on the number of parts.

The simplest form of the knot is the three part, 4 turn, Turk's Head, and it is commenced as shewn in Fig. 276. The standing part is marked *S* and the working part is marked *W*. Take the bight *A* and push it to the left and under the bight *B*, bight *B* being pushed to the right. The working end *W* is carried to the left over bight *B* and under bight *A*.

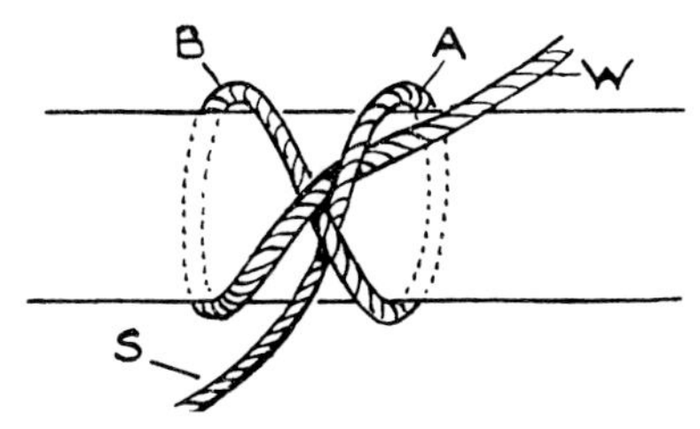

Fig. 276.

This brings *W* and *S* into parallel and the knot is formed. The knot may be doubled, trebled, etc., by following round. This makes a Turk's Head of three parts and four turns (Fig. 277).

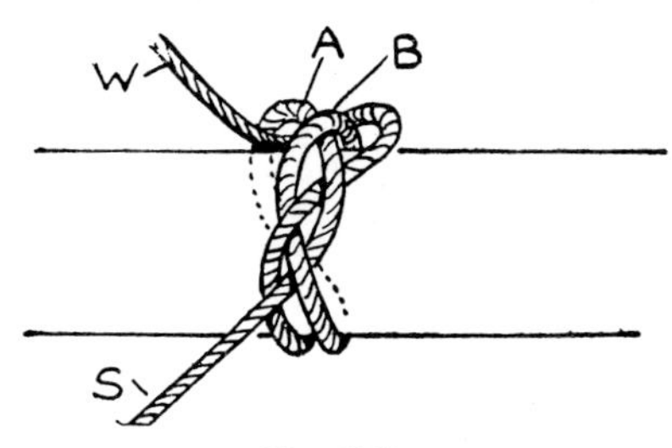

Fig. 277.

Should the object to be covered be large and the chord thin, the number of turns may be increased by pushing bight *A* to the right and bight *B* to the left and tucking *W* again but to the right. Then this process is carried out again in the reverse way, when it will be found that *W* and *S* have again come into parallel. The process may be carried out 2, 4, 6, etc., times and the knot becomes one of 7, 10 turns, etc.

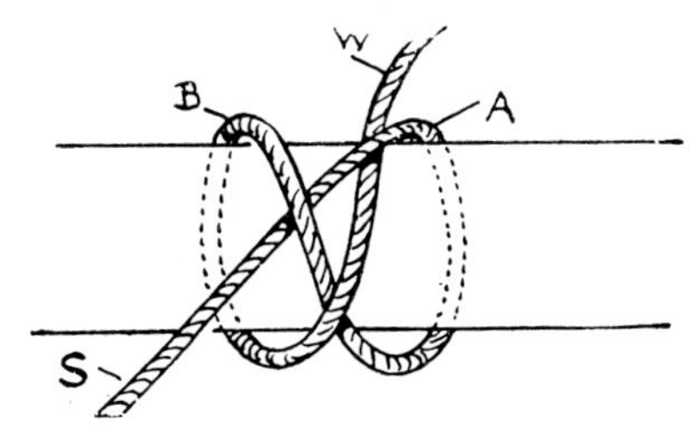

Fig. 278.

If the knot is begun as in Fig. 278, it will be found that the bights *A* and *B* must be thrust under one another and the working end tucked twice before the working and standing ends come into parallel. This will produce a three part, five turn Turk's Head (Fig. 279). The number of turns may be increased as already described.

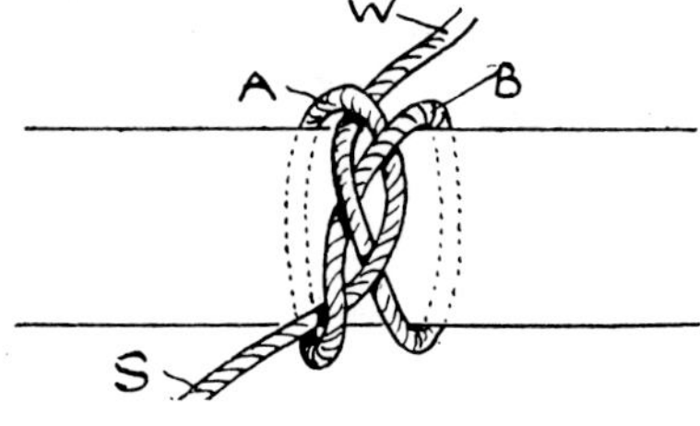

Fig. 279.

The three part Turk's Head followed round twice is shewn in Fig. 280.

Fig. 280.

This completes the Turk's Head of three parts.

Four Part Turk's Head.—Make an Overhand Knot as shewn in Fig. 281. This makes two crosses, *A* and *B.* Carry

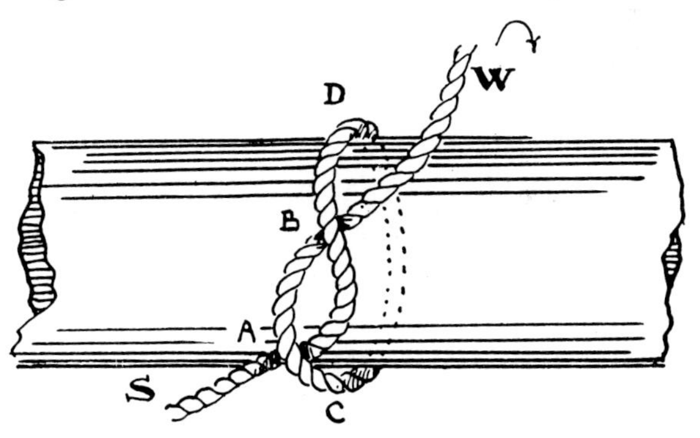

Fig. 281.

on with *W* round the object, coming up at *E*, then under at *F*, over at *G*, over at *H*, and under at *I*. All as shewn in Fig. 282.

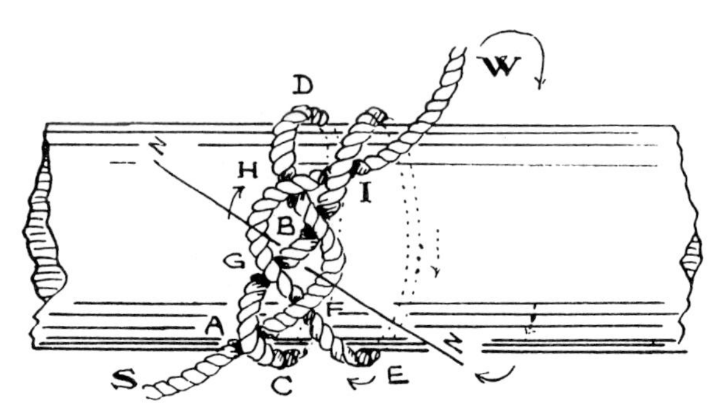

Fig. 282.

Then take *W* round the object again and reeve it again along the line *Z*—*Z* from right to left, over, under, and over.

This completes a Four Part Knot of three turns.

Turk's Head of Five Parts.—Begin the five part Turk's Head as in Fig. 283.

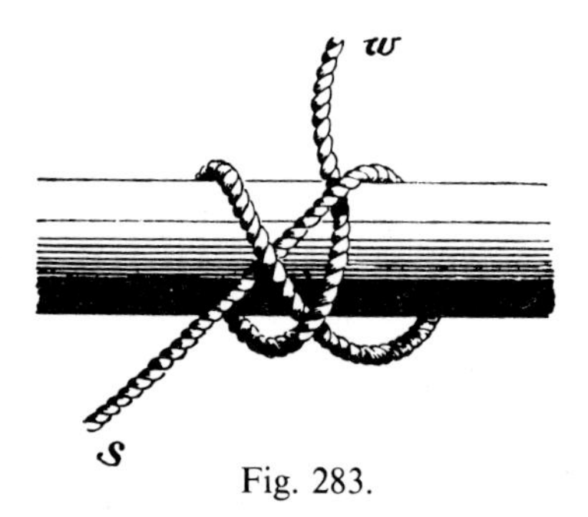

Fig. 283.

To get to the second stage, shewn in Fig. 284, the working end *w* is passed right round, crossing at the back of the knot over the dotted strand *b* and is tucked alongside the standing end in front of the knot. It is again passed round and this time it is tucked under the dotted strand *b* and over the dotted strand *c* at the back of the knot. This gives Fig. 284.

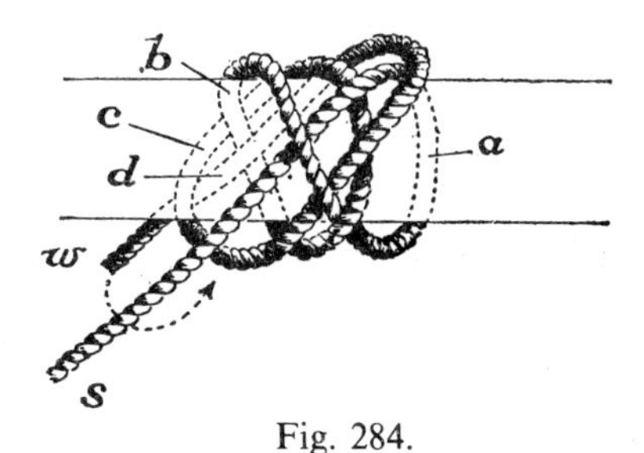

Fig. 284.

To get to the third stage, shewn in Fig. 285, the working end *w* as shewn in Fig. 284 is brought up against the standing end but is tucked in the opposite way as shewn in Fig. 285

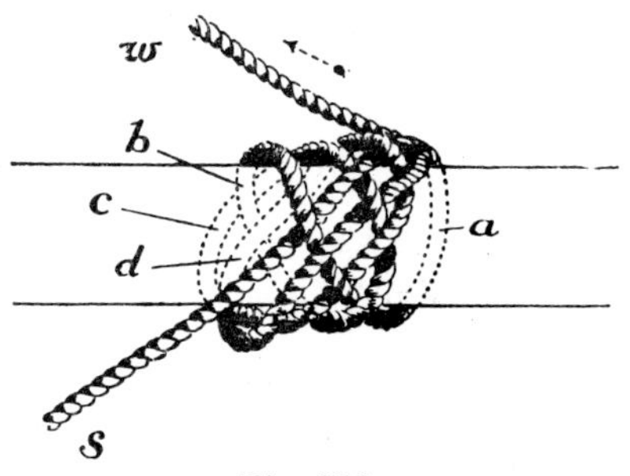

Fig. 285.

(*i.e.* where the standing end crosses under a strand, the working end is tucked under and *vice versa*). The last tuck in Fig. 285 is made under the dotted strand *a*.

Fig. 286 shews the back of the knot. The working end *w* is passed over *b* and under *c*.

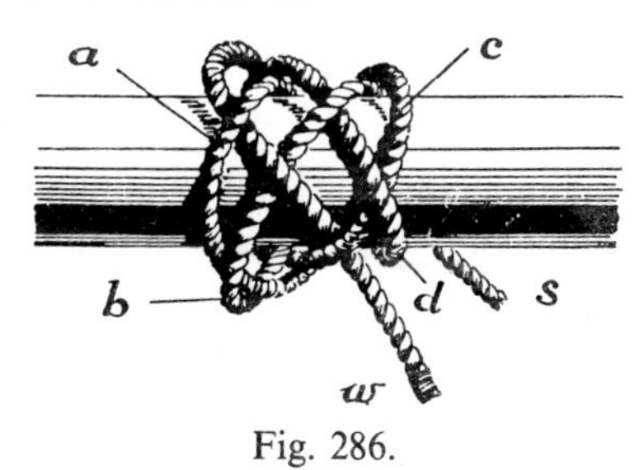

Fig. 286.

Fig. 287 shews the knot with the turns all worked tight. It is usual to follow round till each strand is treble.

Fig. 287.

Nine Parts Turk's Head.—Commence by fastening the standing end of the strand *A* to the rope round which the Turk's Head is to be made, with a turn or two of twine. Then proceed as shewn in Fig. 288.

Pass the strand over the rope at *B*, round the back bringing it to the front at *C* and up again to *D*.

From there it is taken round the back of the rope and returns to the start at *E*. Then carry on over the top of the rope at *F*, round the back, and up between the first and second turns at *G*. Then round in front, over to the back at *H*, and round back to *I* where it turns again. It is now tucked under at *J*, over at *K*, under at *L*, and over at strand *F*. This completes the first stage.

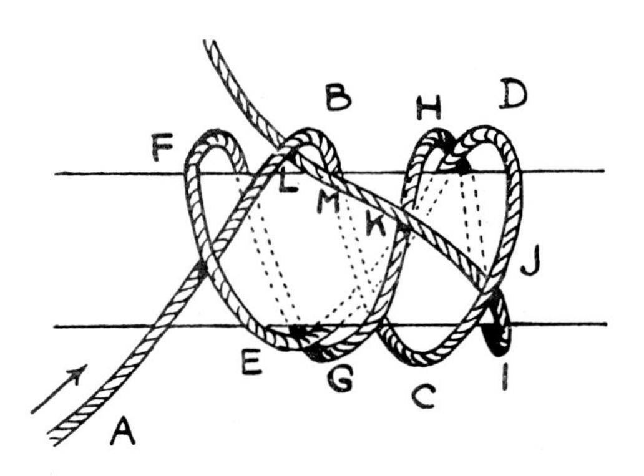

Fig. 288.

The strand is carried round the back, kept to the left of *G*, tucked under *E*, brought up in front, over at *M*, over to the back, under *D E* at the back of the rope, and carried over *H I* to the right of *J*. It is again turned, carried over strand *D C*, keeping to the right of *J*, under the next, then over two, under one, and over one, when it is turned again, carried over the first strand to the right of *A B*, which is the standing end, under the next, keeping parallel with *A B*, over two, under one and over one. This brings it out on the right hand end of the knot. It is turned again, passed under the first strand to the left, and alternately over and under till it reaches the left hand end of the knot.

This completes the groundwork. The rest is simply following round.

Long Turk's Head.—The foregoing paragraphs give empirical methods of making Turk's Heads. I am indebted to Ian A. D. Wilson for the method of making Turk's Heads of any length and number of turns. In the following description the word "turns" is used to indicate the number of times the cord reaches the end of the knot and turns back.

PARTS.—If a line be drawn along the knot from end to end it will cut the parts of the knot. Thus in a three part Turk's Head the line would cut the cord three times, in a five part Turk's Head five times, etc. The number of parts in a Turk's Head indicates the length of the knot.

The Turk's Head can be varied in a number of ways.

1. The original knot can be "followed round" two, three or more times. This is merely a mechanical process.
2. The number of parts can be varied so as to make a knot of any length.
3. The number of turns can be varied.

To make a Long Turk's Head.—Take a piece of cord of the required length (which can be learned only by experience) as it depends on the diameter of the object to be covered and the length of the Turk's Head desired, and with one or two turns of twine stopper the middle of it on to the object to be covered. One half of the cord may be neglected meantime: it may be called the "standing end". Take the other, or "working end" a number of times round the object to be covered as in Fig. 289, the standing end being *S* and the working end *W*. The number of times the cord is taken round the object depends on the length of the knot required and also the skill of the operator.

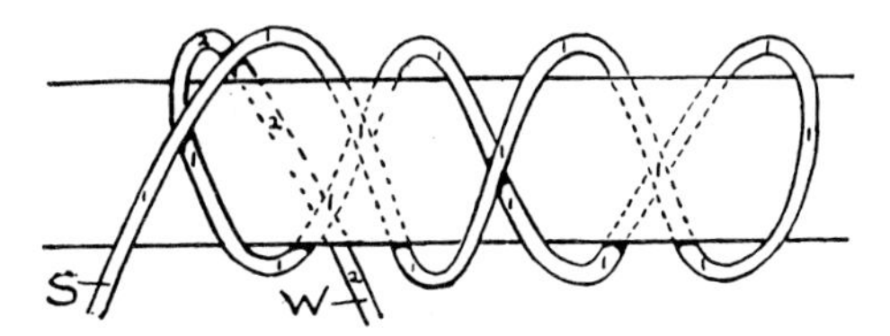

Fig. 289.

It will be noticed that in returning from the right to the left end of the knot the cord at each crossing is taken alternately over and under the preceding lay. This completes the first turn (Fig. 289).

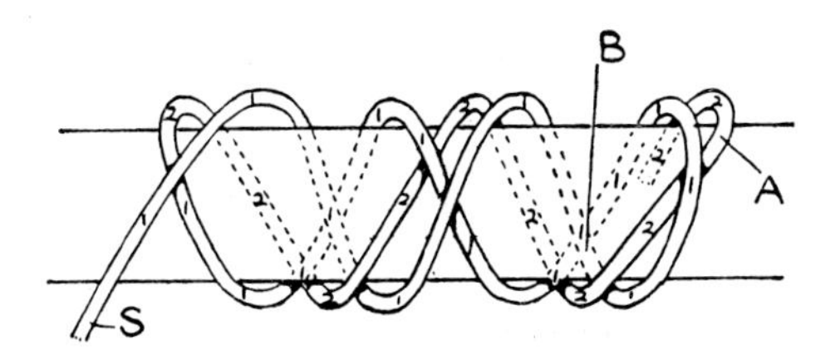

Fig. 290.

The working end is now carried on round the object again *following closely the preceding lay but being taken over where it went under and vice versa* until it reaches the right end of the knot as shewn in Fig. 290. The working end, in this case, passes under the turn at the end. The working end is now carried on round the object following closely the preceding lay but being taken under and over when the preceding lay was over and under (Fig. 291).

NOTE.—It will be found that, when making the turn at the right hand end, the cord will pass under at *A* and also under at *B* so that it may pass in the reverse way from the preceding lay which it is following. It will be found that this apparent mistake will recur at intervals, but it will come right as the third turn is completed.

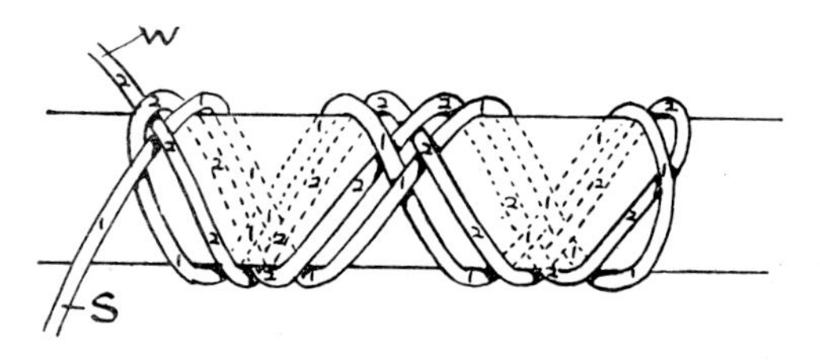

Fig. 291.

The working end is again turned and carried on round the object, closely following the second turn, and again being led over where the second turn goes under and under where the second turn goes over.

When the third turn is completed it will be found that the working end now comes in parallel with the standing end.

On inspection the knot will be found to be symmetrical and, in fact, to be a three turn, 13 part Turk's Head.

The same progress may now be continued until 5, 7, 9, etc., turns have been made.

For clearness the turns have not been shaded but they are numbered 1 and 2. The third turn is not shewn as it would make the diagram too complicated.

The number of turns to be made depends on the diameter of the object to be covered and on the diameter of the cord used, and can best be found by experiment.

The original strand of the knot may now be doubled or trebled by being followed round exactly, that is, going over where the original strand goes over and under where it goes under. It is now that the other half of the cord may be used for this purpose after the twine stopping has been removed.

For a Turk's Head with rosettes, see "Ocean Plait or Oval Mat" (Fig. 312).

A Long Turk's Head made using "Studs".—Captain E. W. Denison, R.N., gives the following method of making a Long Turk's Head.

The knot is made by taking one or more turns round the object before reaching the far end and returning. It is possible to make it with an even or an uneven number of turns (at the ends of the knot).

To make it with the number of "turns" required (which will vary with the size of object to be covered and of the line to be used), provide the same number of studs as "turns" at each end. These studs are driven into the object and equally spaced round it.

Begin at any stud on the left. Take any number of turns

as desired round the object in the direction as shewn by the arrows in the figure. Go round the stud on the opposite side at the other end, return with the same number of round turns to the next stud at the starting end.

If you are using an even number of studs at each end always make a succession of overs on the return route. If you are using an uneven number of studs make alternate overs and unders.

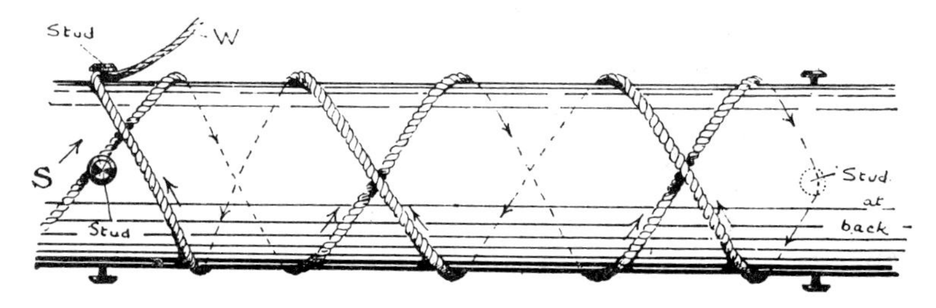

Fig. 292.

In either case after this you merely do exactly opposite to what you did in the preceding turn, *i.e.* make an over where you previously made an under and *vice versa*. You will find that you frequently have to make two overs or two unders in succession, but this corrects itself later. When the knot is completed it can be followed round one or more times as desired.

In the figure the working end is marked *W* and the standing end *S* (Fig. 292).

Turk's Head made on a "Former". When making or describing a Turk's Head Knót of more than three plys there is always a difficulty in illustrating the back of the knot, remembering the tucks when making the knot, and keeping them in place while doing another tuck. Mr. Alexander has evolved a method which gets over these difficulties.

Some of the things in favour of his plan are:— The nails or pins are not driven into the object to be covered so that the knot may be made round a metal bar.

The whole of the tucks and turns are in sight and there is no fear of them coming adrift during the work.

The job is done on a "Former" which, for a knot of, say, seven plys using ordinary cord, need not be bigger than 4 inches by 4 inches.

Into this are set, slackly so as to be easily withdrawn, twelve nails or pegs as shewn in Fig. 293 and the "Former" is lashed to the object to be covered as shewn in Fig. 294.

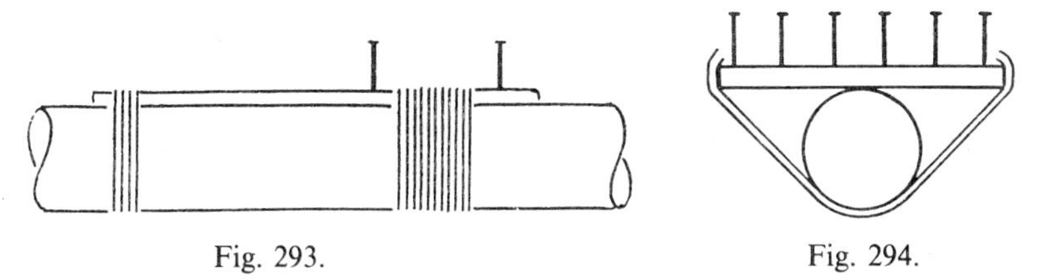

Fig. 293. Fig. 294.

Fig. 295 and 296 shew the start of the knot and Fig. 297 the complete knot ready for doubling.

The nails or pegs are now drawn, the lashings cut and the "Former" removed. This leaves the knot loose so the next job is to tighten it up and then double or treble it.

Each cord as it disappears at the top goes straight round the back and reappears at the bottom as shewn.

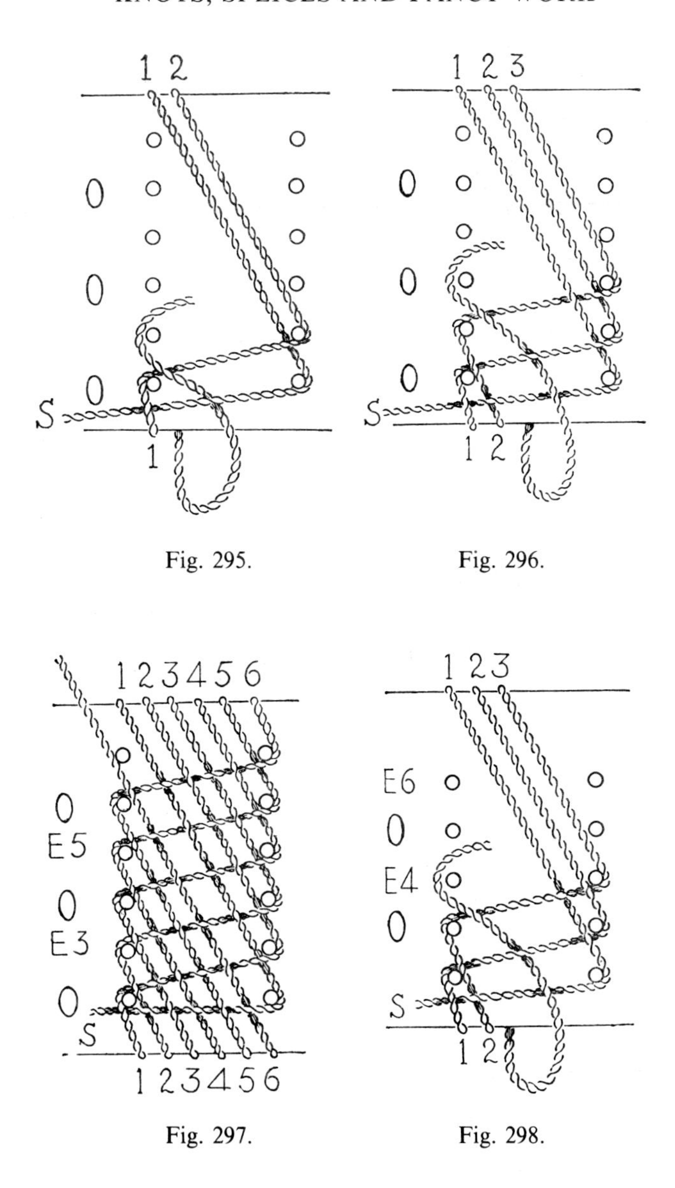

Fig. 295.

Fig. 296.

Fig. 297.

Fig. 298.

If weaving stops at peg *E*3 (Fig. 298.) a simple three part knot is made, if stopped at *E*4 a five part knot.

There are some simple rules to remember. At the odd pegs at the Left, marked *O* for over, the working end passes *over* two cords in succession. See Fig. 297. All the rest is plain weave, over and under, and the whole thing is plain in view.

In making Knots of an even number of turns the *Even* pegs should be marked *O* for overs as in Fig. 298.

Herringbone Weave.—Take six or eight long strands. Lay them along the article to be covered, middle them and

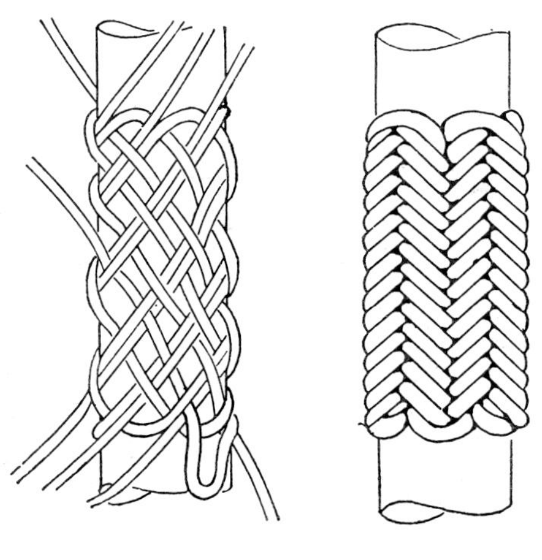

Fig. 299. Fig. 300.

seize them at each end of the space to be covered after making a 45 degree helix.

Tuck the lower ends up and to the Right over one and under one to the rim.

Turn end for end and do the same with the other set of legs. The Right diagonals will now be double and the Left Diagonals single as appears in the first diagram. Fig. 299.

Turn end for end and do the same with the other set of legs.

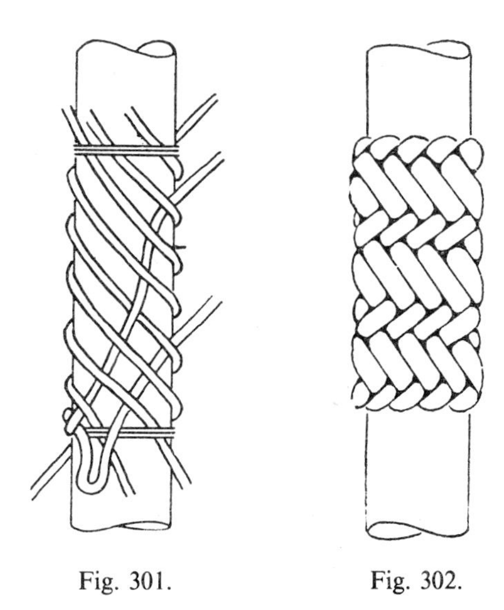

Fig. 301. Fig. 302.

Continue to stick all the legs over two and under two until they meet. Scatter the ends well and, finally, stick opposing legs under the same two parts, cut the seizings, draw up the knot evenly, scatter the ends and trim them. This makes Herringboning that runs with the width of the knot.

Herringbone Weave.—Another pattern. Middle and seize a group of legs sufficient in number to fit closely together round the object to be covered. After the legs have been helixed and seized a second time at the bottom, take the set of lower legs and stick each one to the Right over one strand and under three strands then over one and under three again. Turn the work end for end and tuck each strand over one and under three, and continue to tuck over one and under three until the two sets meet, where care must be taken that the over one and under three sequence is unbroken. Then ends to be well scattered and trimmed. Fig. 301 and 302.

Other weaves may be made by this method such as over two and under two, or over two and under three, etc.

PLAITS.

The simplest plait is the "Chain Plait", sometimes called "Drummer's Plait". It can be used to shorten a rope.

To form it proceed as though you are going to make an ordinary overhand knot, but instead of working with both ends use the end and a bight as in Fig. 302.

This will form the loop *a* (Fig. 302), through which pass a bight of *B* and continue in this way until all the slack rope is used up, and it must be finished off by running the end through the last loop (Fig. 303).

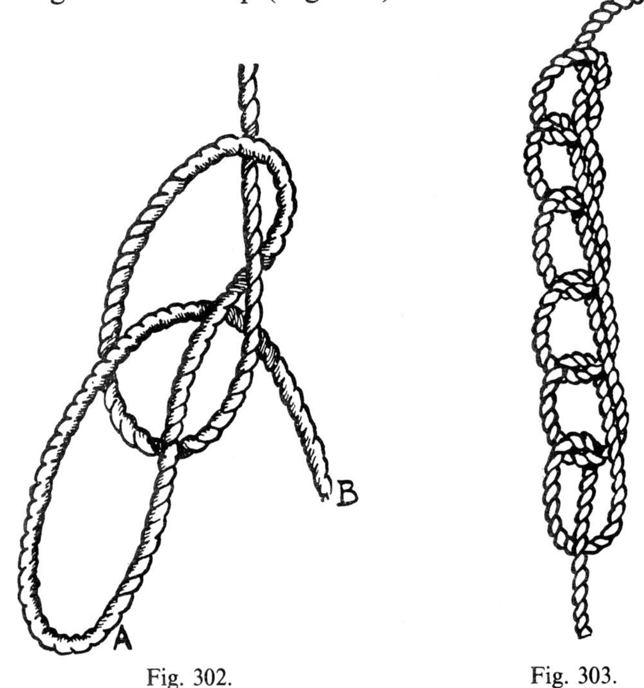

Fig. 302.

Fig. 303.

Double Chain.—The Double Chain is a little more intricate than the Chain Knot, and is formed by taking a turn round the standing part and thus forming a loop *C* through which the end *A* is passed, thus forming the loop *B* (Fig. 304).

The end *A* is brought back and dipped down through *B* and this is continued as long as required, finishing off by running the end through the last bight and hauling it taut (Fig. 305).

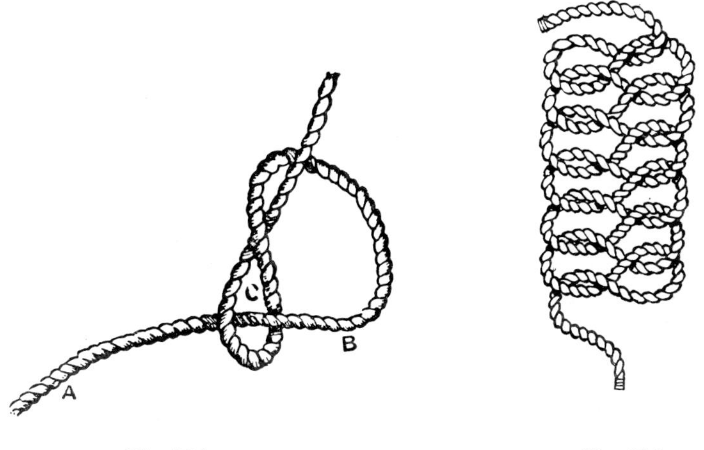

Fig. 304.

Fig. 305.

Twist or Plait Knot.—Another method of shortening a small handy rope is known as the Twist or Plait Knot.

Arrange the rope in such a manner that the amount to be taken up forms a bight as in Fig. 306.

Then by taking *A* over *B* and *C* over *A, B* over *C, A* over

B, and so on, taking the outside one on each side alternately over the middle one, the plait is formed. To keep the plait clear the end has to be continually dipped through the first bight made (Fig. 307).

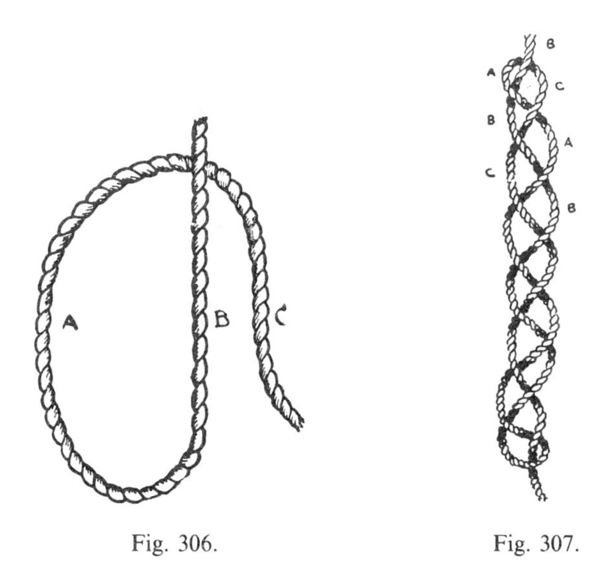

Fig. 306. Fig. 307.

Square Plait.—This plait looks exactly like square sennit made with eight parts.

Begin by throwing on an ordinary Thumb Knot loop as shewn in Fig. 308, thus forming loop *a*.

Pass the working end *w* back through the Thumb Knot, thus forming loop *b* (Fig. 309).

Then with the working end *w* form loop *c* through loop *a* as shewn in Fig. 310.

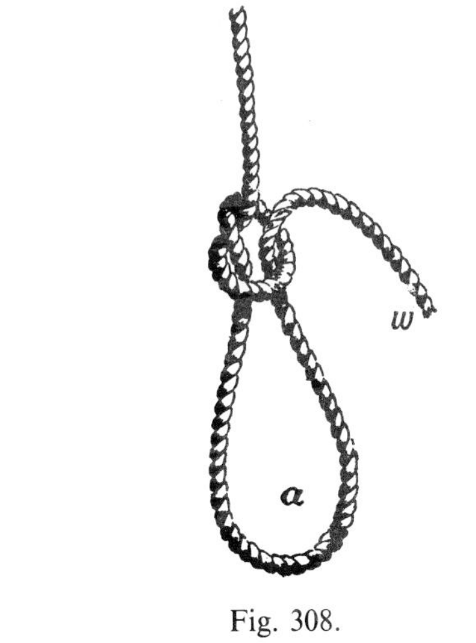

Fig. 308.

Fig. 309.

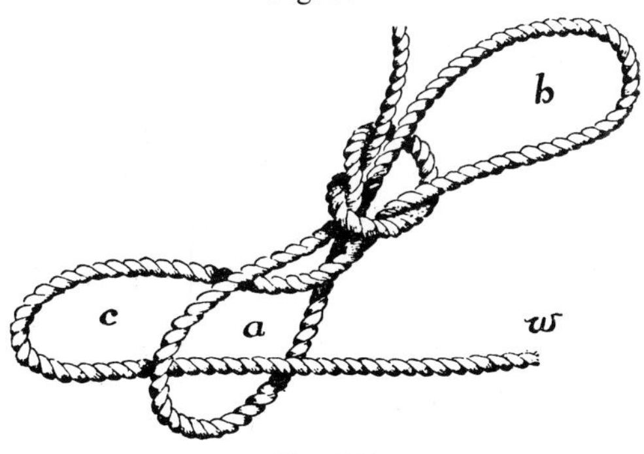

Fig. 310.

Draw loop *a* tight by pulling the upper side of loop *b*. This will leave you with two loops *b* and *c*.

With the working end *w* form a loop through loop *b* in the same way as you did through loop *a*.

Draw loop *b* tight by pulling the upper side of loop *c* and proceed making loops alternately. Finish by passing the end down through the left-hand loop (Fig. 311) up through the right-hand loop and down between the last two middle strands. Pull taut.

Fig. 311.

Ocean Plaits or Mats—Oval Mat.—It was often used as a fancy knife lanyard. Start as in Fig. 312. (If the Plait is to be on a lanyard the loop at *a* must be left long). Then holding the knot in the left hand, palm up, make bight *b* round the

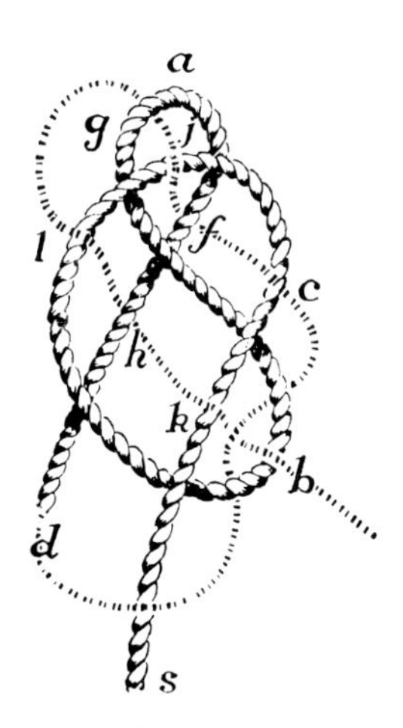

Fig. 312.

third finger and *c* round the first finger laying the end *s* down to the left. Or lay out the line on a table as shewn by the shaded part of Fig. 312. Now carry the working end *d* over the standing end *s* under bight *b* over at *c*, under *f* over at *j*, down through bight *a* and under *g*, round by the left, over at *l*, under *h* and over *k*. Now the part that was taken under bight *b* has to be pulled up through that bight and the end *d* rove through it. The dotted line indicates all this.

When all the parts are worked in taut and flat it appears as in Fig. 313. If the bight *a* be pulled in as indicated by the dotted lines at *x*, and the free ends rove round each following the other till two or three parts are completed a very pleasing design results. This is called the "Oval Mat" (Fig. 314). The figure shews the "carrying round" done once only: it may, of course, be done several times.

Fig. 313.

Fig. 314.

If a rope, etc., be threaded through the centre "hole" (Fig. 314), and the knot then worked tight round the rope and "followed round", a very nice collar is produced like a three part Turk's Head with "rosettes", one at the front and the other at the back (Fig. 315).

Fig. 315.

Another Method of Making the Oval or Long Mat.—Begin as in Fig. 316. This is a 3-part Turk's Head, Fig. 323, with the lower loops pulled out.

Loop *C* is then crossed, right handed, and laid over to the right, and loop *D* is crossed, right handed, and laid over loop *C* to the left as in Fig. 317.

End *A* is led down and tucked, as shewn in Fig. 318.

End *B* is led down and tucked in a similar way.

If the end *A* be now brought in and led back parallel to *B* and followed round, and end *B* led back parallel to *A* and followed round, the mat is complete.

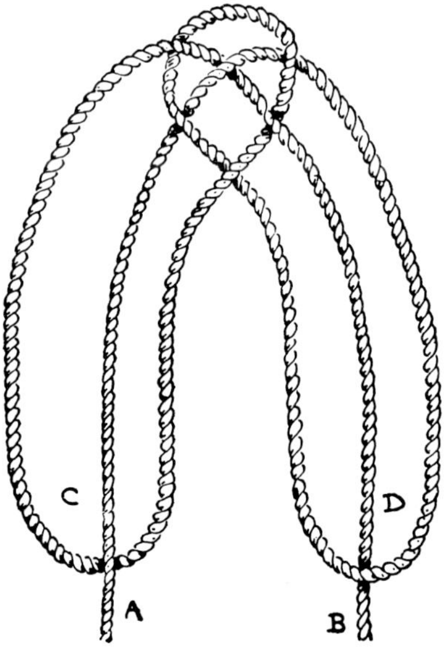

Fig. 316.

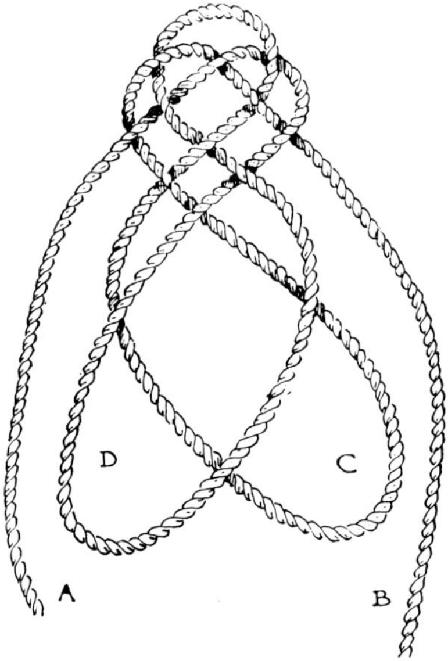

Fig. 317.

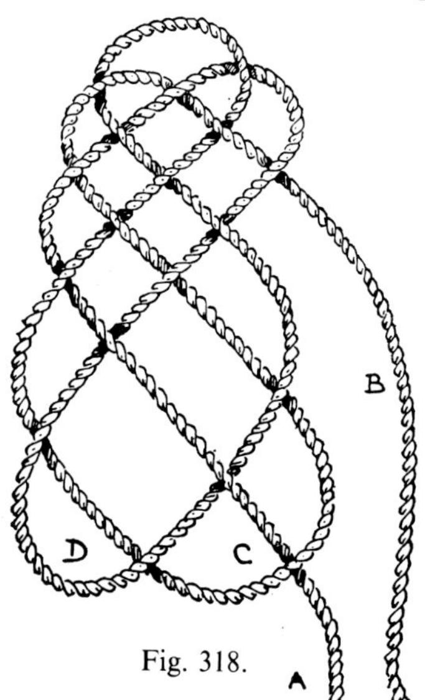

Fig. 318.

This mat may be made of any length, if the loops and ends are long enough, by continuing to cross the loops, laying them over as before, and tucking the ends.

Square Mat or Ocean Plait.—The "Square Mat" or "Ocean Plait" is commenced as shewn in Fig. 319.

Now reeve the bight *A* over *B* and under *C*.

Then make a bight *E* on the other end as shewn in Fig. 320, pass it under the first end, over at *D*, under at *B*, over at *C* and under at *A*.

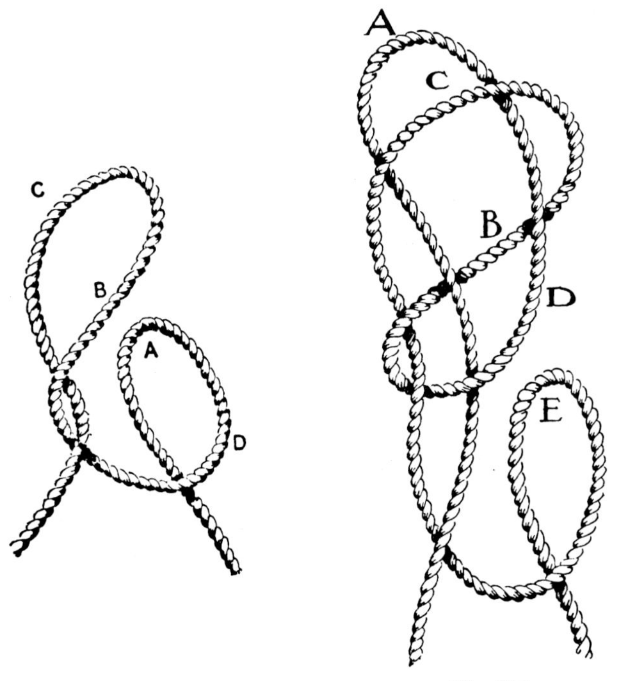

Fig. 319. Fig. 320.

Repeat this process as often as desired using each end alternately and finish off by bringing one end, not doubled into a bight, under the other end, round to the right; over the lowest bight and up the middle, going under and over alternately till the working end emerges at the top of the knot (Fig. 321).

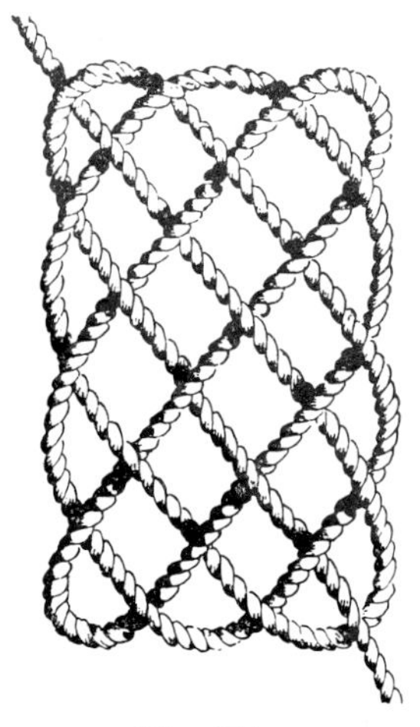

Fig. 321.

Carrick Mat.—This is based on a Double Carrick Knot, but whereas in an ordinary Double Carrick the ends come out on opposite sides of the knot, they are required, for this knot to come out on the same side. This is achieved by starting as in Fig. 322.

Then *a* is passed over *b*, under *c*, over *d*, under *e* and over *f* when the knot will appear as in Fig. 323.

Fig. 322.

Then by pulling in the bight *x* and following round each end by the other the result will be as Fig. 324. This is really a flattened out Turk's Head.

Fig. 323. Fig. 324.

Carrick Mat.—As shewn in Fig. 325, this is a four-sided Mat and it is a flattened out three part Turk's Head of four plats. It can only produce one size of mat when using any one size of cord or rope. In order to make a Carrick Mat of any convenient size from one size of cord begin by making a Turk's Head of three parts round a spindle of, say, 5-inch diameter and make the Turk's Head of any convenient number of plats. Then take it off the spindle and flatten it out. Follow round inside the first parts, say twice. This makes a mat with a hole in the centre. This hole may now be

Fig. 325.

filled in by making another flattened out Turk's Head interlaced with the first. The easiest way to do this is to make,

Fig. 326.

on a separate piece of cord, a very loose Turk's Head of half the number of plats of the original Turk's Head, flatten it out, and carefully reproduce it with the end of the cord in the centre of the mat. Fig. 325 shews a three part Turk's Head of 10 plats made on a spindle 5-inch diameter. It is made of fishing line about 3/16-inch diameter. The mat is 6-inch diameter. The centre part is a Turk's Head of 5 plats.

Another variation of the Carrick Mat can be made by commencing with a five part Turk's Head round a spindle and flattening it out and then following round in the usual way.

Fig. 326 shews a mat made with a five part Turk's Head on a 3-inch spindle out of ¾-inch rope, that is ¼-inch diameter.

The resulting mat is 5¾-inch diameter.

Jury Knot Mats.—The basis of these is the Jury Knot. There are a number of variants. For instance, the number of loops used. The illustrations shew mats made using four loops and five loops.

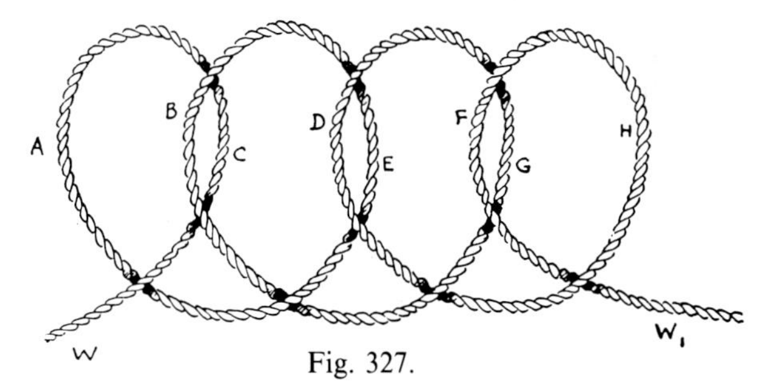

Fig. 327.

Fig. 327 shews the four loops and two ends. Catch *D* and draw it under *C*, over *B*, and under *A*; and catch *E* and draw it over *F*, under *G*, and over *H*. The result, flattened out, is shewn in Fig. 328.

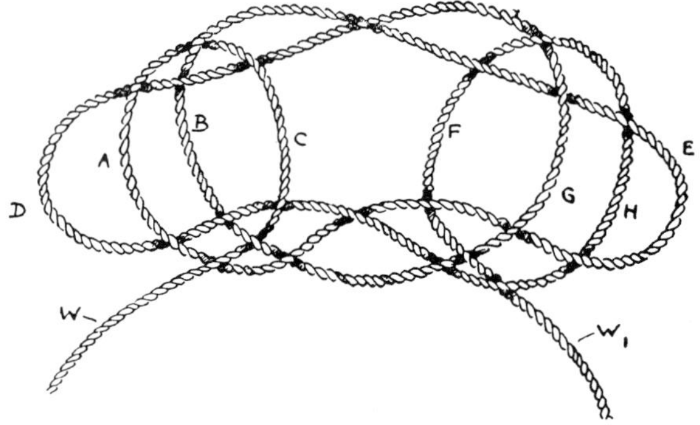

Fig. 328.

The two loops *C* and *F* are now drawn in towards one another and *F* is lapped over *C*. The end *W* is then led round, as shewn shaded, under *D*, over *A*, under *B*, over *F* and under *C* (Fig. 329).

The end W_1 is led in a similar way (not shewn so as not

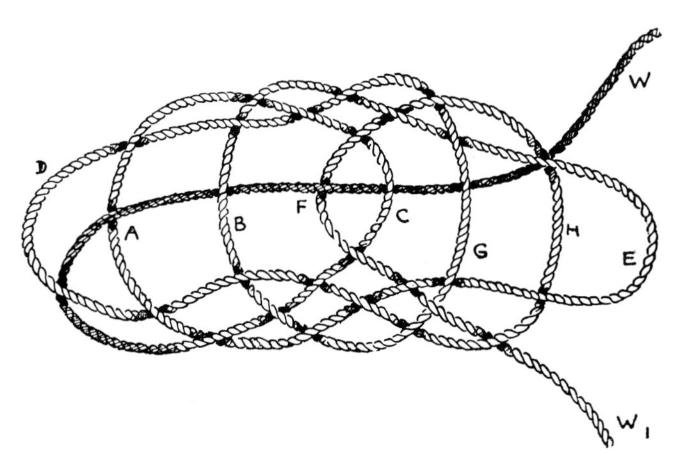

Fig. 329.

to complicate the figure too much) over *E*, under *H*, over *G*, under *C*, and over *F*.

This brings the two ends *W* and W_1 parallel and completes the foundation of the mat. To finish the mat, the ends simply follow round so as to double or treble the strands.

Jury Knot Mat of Five Loops.—Begin by making the five loops as in Fig. 330. Then draw out loops *C* and *H* as shown till they are long enough to reach the opposite end of the knot and pass *C* under *D* and over *E*. Pass *H* over *G* and under *F*.

This brings them out at the centre of the knot. Loop *C* is now passed upwards through loop *H*, over *F*, under *G*, over *I* and under *J*.

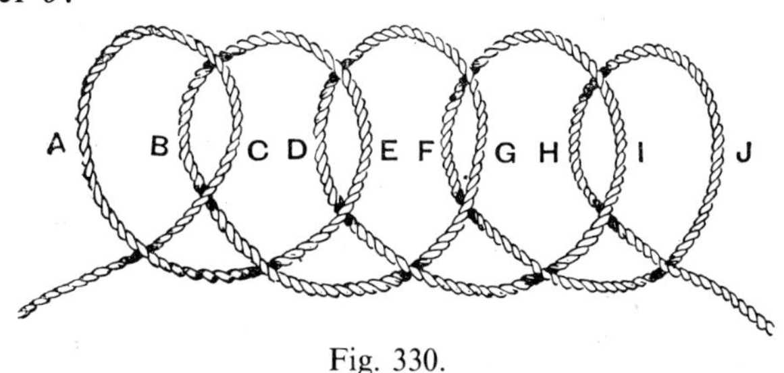

Fig. 330.

And loop*H* is passed downwards through loop *C*, under *E*, over *D*, under *B* and over *A*. This gives Fig. 331.

The procedure is now the same as for the Four Loop Mat. W_1 is led round (shewn shaded) under *C*, over *J*, under *I*, over *G*, and under *F*. *W* is led round and over *H*, under *A*, over *B*, under *D*, and over *E*.

This brings the two ends *W* and W_1 parallel and

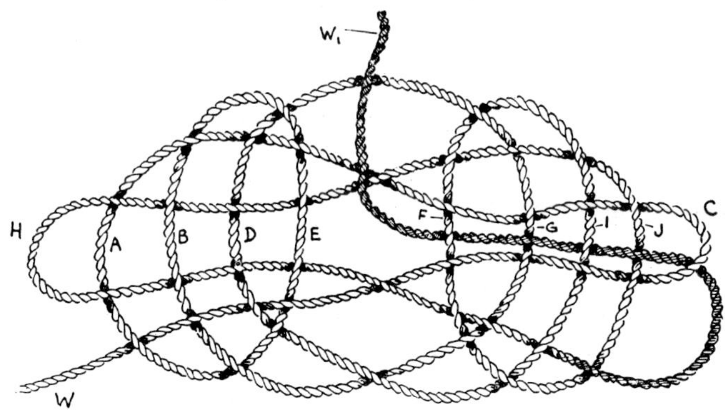

Fig. 331.

completes the foundation of the mat. To finish the mat the ends simply follow round so as to double or treble the strands.

Woven or Sword Mat.—This may be made in various ways which differ in details, but the principle is shown in Figs. 332 and 333. The method is to make a primitive loom.

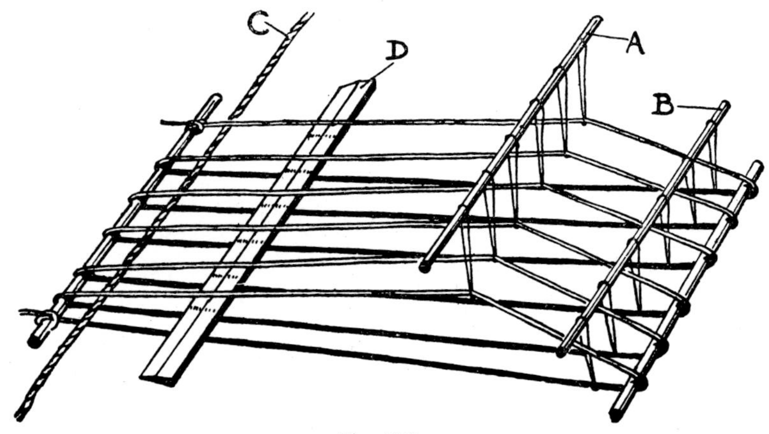

Fig. 332.

Two bars or tightly stretched ropes are fixed at a distance apart the length of the required mat.

On them is wound the rope which is to form the warp.

Two pieces of wood, *A* and *B*, are laid across the warp. *A* is connected to every alternate line of warp by means of loose loops of yarn, and *B* is similarly connected to the other lines of warp as shown in the figure.

By lifting *A*, every alternate line of warp is lifted and the weft *C*, is passed. It is then pressed home by the sword *D*.

This is a flat piece of wood usually slightly bevelled on one edge.

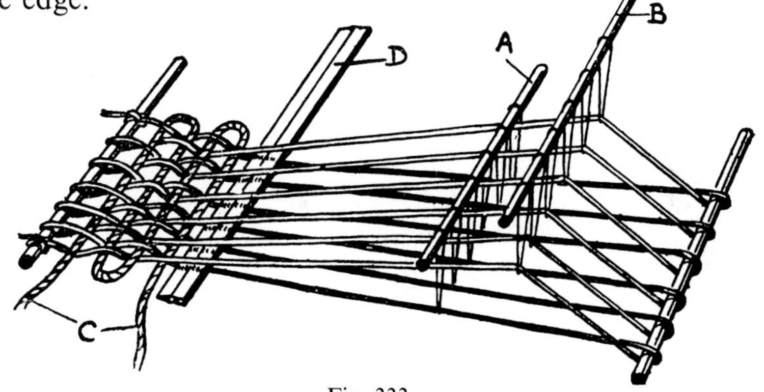

Fig. 333.

The sword is withdrawn, *A* is lowered and *B* is raised, bringing with it the other series of warped lines. The weft is passed back and pushed home by the sword as before. This process is continued until the mat is finished. At the end there will be no room for the sword so the weft must be got in by using a marline-spike.

Wrought Mat or Paunch Mat.—Fig. 334. The earliest and the best description of this mat that I have found is in Darcy Lever's *Young Sea Officer's Sheet Anchor* of 1819.

A piece of Hambro' line is stretched in a horizontal direction, as in the figure; and foxes, according to the breadth intended, are hung over it. The fox nearest the left hand *c* has a turn twisted in its two parts, and one part is given to the man opposite (two people being employed). The next fox *d* has also a turn twisted in its two parts, and one

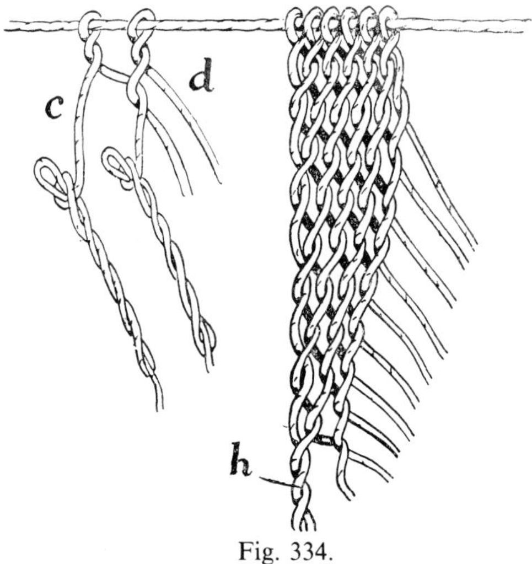

Fig. 334.

part given back: the remaining end is twisted round the first which was given back (as in figure) and that again round its own part. Proceeding in this manner with the other foxes, the mat will appear in the working as shewn in the figure, until the whole of the foxes are put in. The two to the left *h* are always twisted together, till those to the right hand are worked to them, in order to keep in the turns each time. At the bottom another piece of Hambro' line is put in: the ends of the foxes split, and hitched round it, then put through the other twists with a marline-spike.

To render the surface of these mats softer, strands of old rope are cut in pieces of about 3 inches in length, pushed through the divisions of the twists, and then opened out. These yarns ar called "thrums".

Russian Mat or Sennit.—Take a piece of cordage of sufficient weight and length and secure it to two belaying pins or other convenient fastenings. Take a number of strands suitable to the width of the mat required. Middle the

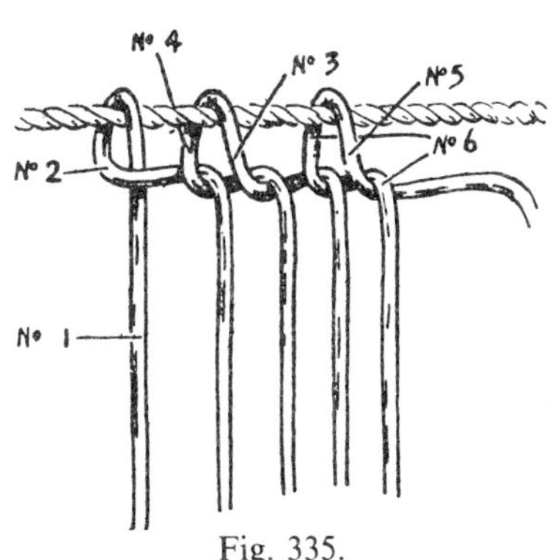

Fig. 335.

strands over the lashing (Fig. 335). In the figure the strands have been numbered; the front part of the first strand No. 1, back part of same strand No. 2, front part of next strand No. 3, back part No, 4, etc.

Begin at your left hand. Take up No. 2 up on the left and over No. 1. Then No. 4 over No. 2, the No. 3 over No. 4, No. 6 over No. 3, No. 5 over No. 6 and continue back and front right across. This is shewn in Fig. 335.

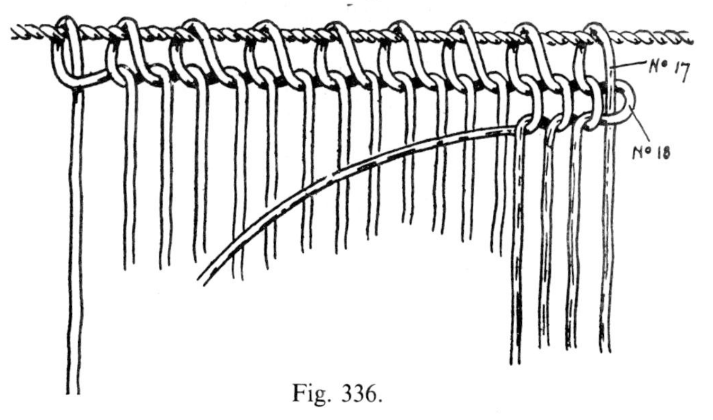

Fig. 336.

Fig. 336 shews the next stage. Take the last strand No. 17 over No. 18, and bring No. 18 around over No. 17. Then take the first strand to the left over and under No. 18. Take the next strand on the left over and under the one brought in, and so continue across. The right and left front strands, Nos. 1 and 17, will remain the side strands throughout. If they are of sufficient length they may be knotted behind the back of the operator. The mat may be made with temporary side strands of the same weight as the lacing; these can be removed in the process of lacing. The lacing can then be rove through the loops.

To finish the mat, take the side strands across the bottom of the mat (or put in another lashing), hitch all the strands around the side strands, bring the ends out at the back and tuck twice up through the back of the mat (Fig. 337).

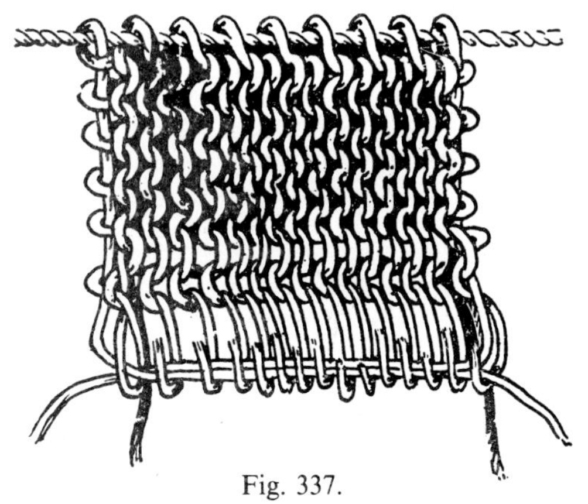

Fig. 337.

Cockscombing.—This was often used to cover a ring, a spindle eye, etc.

Cockscombing using One Part.—Put on half hitches alternately to the right and left as in Fig. 338.

Fig. 338.

Cockscombing, using Three or any odd number of parts.—Stopper the required number of parts on to the heart. Fig. 339 shews three parts. Then lay on half hitches with each part in succession alternately to right and to left always using the farthest back part.

The number of parts to be used depends on the size of the heart and of the parts or strands used. The more parts used the wider becomes the pointed "comb".

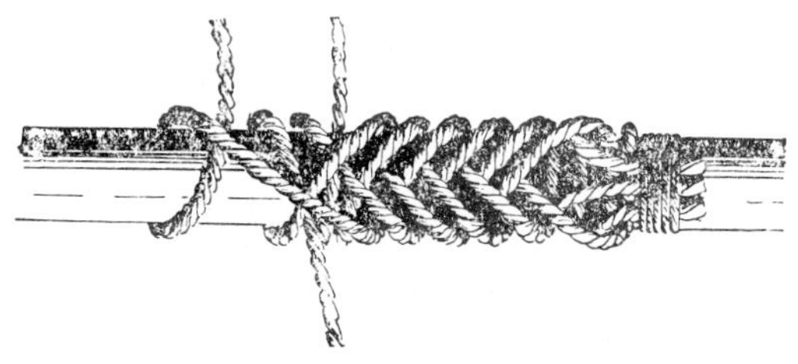

Fig. 339.

Many variations may be made by making different numbers of hitches to the Right and then to the Left.

A Rose Lashing.—This lashing is used for securing a rope with eyes in the ends round a mast or spar.

Through one eye a lanyard is spliced and this is passed crossways over and under one eye and then over and under the other. The end is then taken round the crossings, and tucked (Fig. 340).

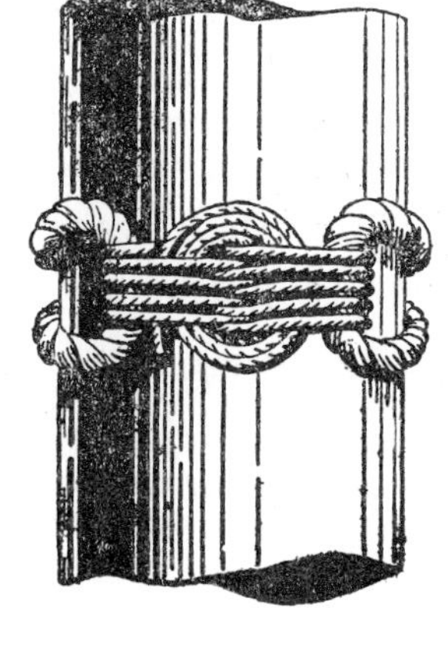

Fig. 340.

A Hammock Clew.—Take twelve lengths of spurnyarn or light stuff, middle them and seize them together in the form of an eye, which may be finished with cockscombing.

Divide the yarns half up and half down. Take the outer yarn on each side across so as to form the filling or warp and leave the ends sticking out. Cross the remaining yarns over this filling. Bring the two outer yarns across and leave the ends sticking out and repeat. The two last yarns are knotted together (Fig. 341).

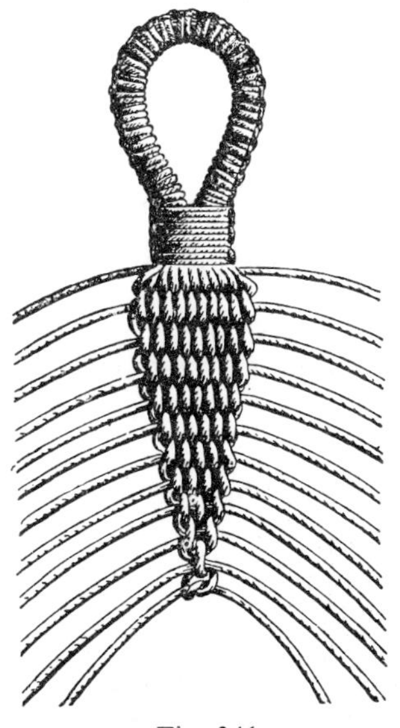

Fig. 341.

Puddening an Anchor Ring.—This is how the job was described in 1819 by Darcy Lever in his book, *The Young Sea Officer's Sheet Anchor*. Probably Mr. Chucks, the boatswain—later Count Chucksen—would have used different language!

"The ring of the anchor is well parcelled with tarred canvas and then wrapped round with twice-laid stuff which is called 'puddening the anchor'. It is done thus:

"A number of lengths are cut, each three times the diameter of the ring. These are laid on the ring and stopped by a temporary seizing in the middle *a*. They are laid by hand as far as *b* when a turn or two of ratline stuff is taken round and a heaver, *b*, being put through it, it is hove well round, which stretches all the turns of the pudding or wreath, making them lie taut and even (Fig. 342). A seizing is clapped on within the heaver and snaked, the heaver is then taken off.

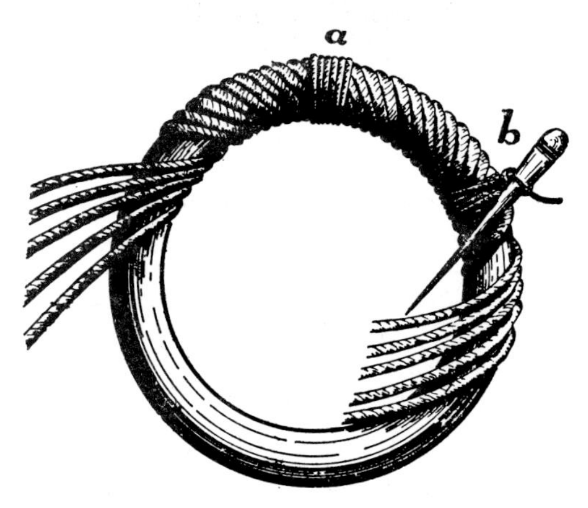

Fig. 342.

"The parts are then laid and hove in the same manner to

c (Fig. 343) where another seizing is clapped on. The same operation is performed on the other side to *d* and *e*, when it will appear like the figure (Fig.343), the temporary seizing being taken off. The ends of the pudding are then opened out (*f*) and well tarred".

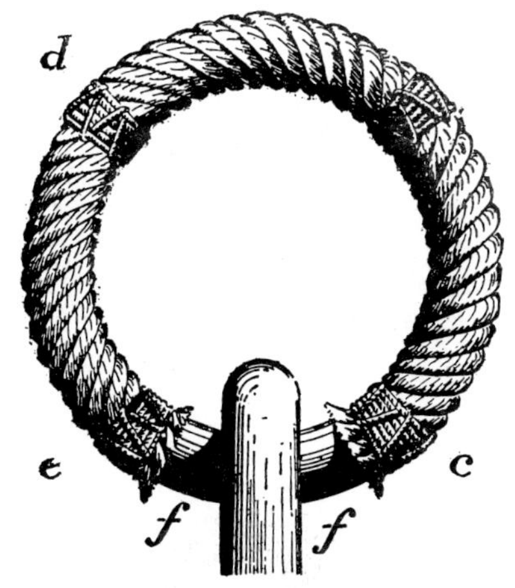

Fig. 343.

A Selvagee.—This consists of a hank of tarred marline or spurnyarn stoppered at intervals as shewn in 1 (Fig. 344).

It is used to attach one of the blocks of a tackle to a rope. For instance, it would be used round a shroud to attach the upper block of a tackle for setting up the lanyard.

In the same figure, 2 shews the Selvagee middled round the shroud. The bights *A* and *B* are then brought across in front of the shroud, taking *A* through *B* as shewn in 3.

Continue to wind the bights round the shroud, again

taking *A* through *B* (at the back of the shroud this time) thus making 4. The block of the tackle is hooked through the bights *A* and *B* in front of the shroud.

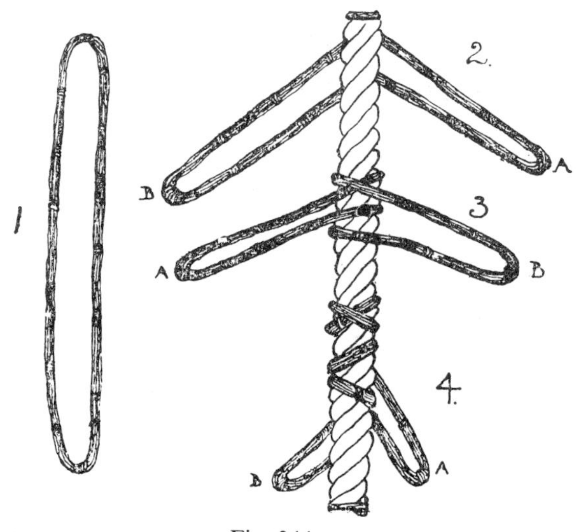

Fig. 344.

Grafting.—Properly speaking this is a method of joining two ropes but the name is often applied to the method used in pointing a rope, covering a mouse on a stay, or a fender, etc., as the process is the same in each case.

Grafting is done by unlaying the ends of the ropes to be joined, marrying them as for a splice and stopping them at the join. The strands are then opened out and the yarns laid up into nettles, as for pointing. Alternate nettles of one rope are then laid along the other rope and two or three turns of twine, the last turn hitched, are passed round them as in pointing. The other lot of nettles are then brought down (and the first lot laid back) and seized, and so on until a sufficient length is worked. The nettles of the other rope are then worked in the same way.

It is a laborious way of joining two ropes and it is not very satisfactory as it is not a strong joint.

What is also called Grafting is done by stopping a sufficient number of nettles or yarns round a rope. They are then worked over the rope as in pointing. This is sometimes done over the tucks of a splice and it is then called a "Grafted Splice".

Mousing a Hook.—All hooks in running gear should be moused as in Fig. 345. The twine is middled on the shank, turns are taken around tongue and shank on opposite sides. The wrapping turns start at opposite ends, wrapped in opposite directions and are tied in the middle.

Fig. 345.

Securing Lead Line to Lead.—The lead is fitted with a good wire grommet parcelled over. The lead line should have a long eye spliced in it, and is secured by passing the eye through the grommet and over the lead (Fig. 346).

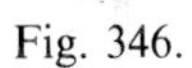

Fig. 346.

Fitting a Flag.—A toggle should be secured at the head of the hoist by an eye splice; a length of rope equal to the width of the flag left below the hoist, as this is the distance the flags should be apart, and then a running eye splice made so as to be rapidly attached to the next flag.

To Stick a Cringle.—First unlay a single strand from the size of rope your cringle is required to be, whip both ends, reeve the strand through the left hand eyelet hole in the sail, having one end longer than the other—nearly a third—keeping the roping of the sail towards you. If a thimble is to be put in the cringle, lay up the parts of the strand together, counting three lays; commence with the short end of the strand towards you, then reeve the long strand from you

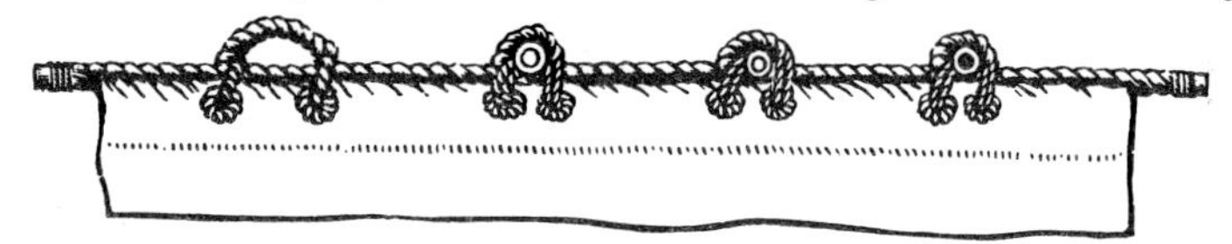

Fig. 347.

through the right hand eyelet hole, taking it through the cringle, and it will be in the right position to lay up in the vacant space left in the cringle; when done, the one end will hang down inside the right hand eyelet hole and the other end outside the left hand one; the ends are then hitched by being rove through their respective eyelet holes and passed over the leech rope and under their own part, one hitch being towards you and the other from you. Then take the ends down under one strand on the right and two on the left of cringle nearest to it; then tuck the ends under the first two strands nearest the hitch, heaving them well in place; the cringle is then fidded out, and the thimble is put in on the fore part of the sail. The ends of the strand are then tucked back, left handed, under one strand, again under two, right handed, as in the first place, heaving them taut in place at each tuck, the ends are then whipped with two of their own yarns and cut off. If a large cringle is needed, count an extra number of lays—5, 7, etc., always an odd number (Fig. 347).

To Finish a Cringle off on the Crown.—Commence as before, but after laying up the strand, instead of forming a hitch with each end, the ends are rove through their respective eyelet holes and tucked back under two strands of the cringles and again laid up as far as the crown, forming a four stranded cringle, and finished off by tucking the ends under two strands and crossing them under the crown of the cringle and cut close off (Fig. 348).

In working a cringle in a piece of rope the only difference is there are no eyelet holes, therefore the strand is tucked under two strands of the rope it is to be worked in.

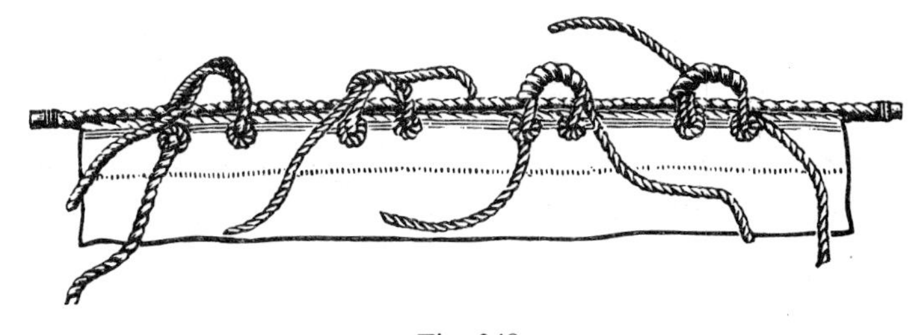

Fig. 348.

To Lengthen a Rope of a Sail with a Single Strand.—Say it is necessary to give a sail one cloth more spread, it would then be necessary to lengthen the head and foot rope. Supposing the width of cloth to be 2 ft. and the size of the rope 3 in. After ripping the rope off four cloths, first of all cut the strand at the distance 2 ft. 6 in. from each other as in Fig. 349.

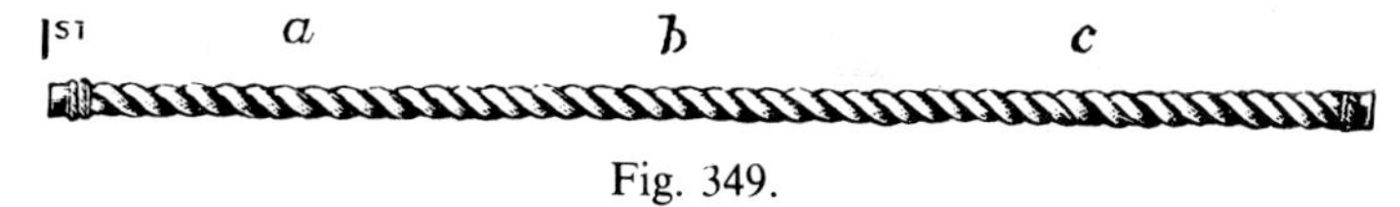

Fig. 349.

Cut one of the strands at *a* and underlay it to *c*, then cut one of the strands remaining at *c* and unlay it to *b*, laying the strand *a* up again as far as *b*; then cut the only remaining strand at *b*, which will be the centre, when your rope will be in two parts. By following the plan the wrong strand cannot possibly be cut. The rope will now appear as in fig. 350.

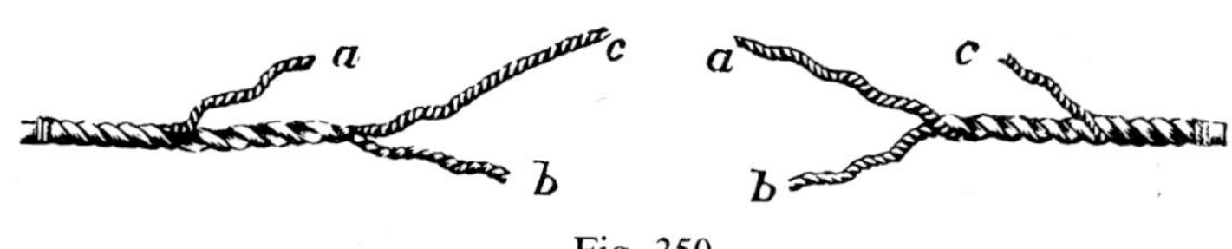

Fig. 350.

Now marry the long end *a* to the end *b*, then lay up the long strand *c* in the lays of the strand *a*, and marry it to the other strand *b* as in Fig. 351.

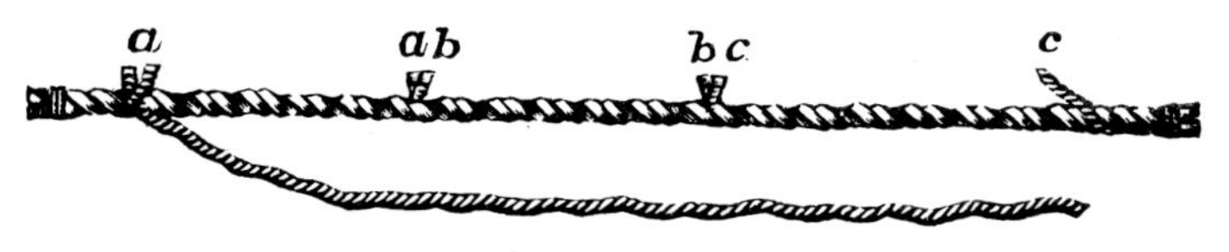

Fig. 351.

Take a strand about 10 ft. in length of the same size rope and marry one end to the short strand *a* as shown above, then fill up the space left from *a* to *c* by laying in the new strand, and marry the other end to the short strand *c*. You will then have four splices to finish off as ordinary long splices (Fig. 352).

Fig. 352.

Jury Knot.—The Jury Knot is useful when a jury mast has to be rigged, as the loops form a means of attaching the necessary supports to the mast. The centre *K* (Fig. 354) is slipped over the masthead, and the weight brought on the stays tightens it and holds it in its position on the mast.

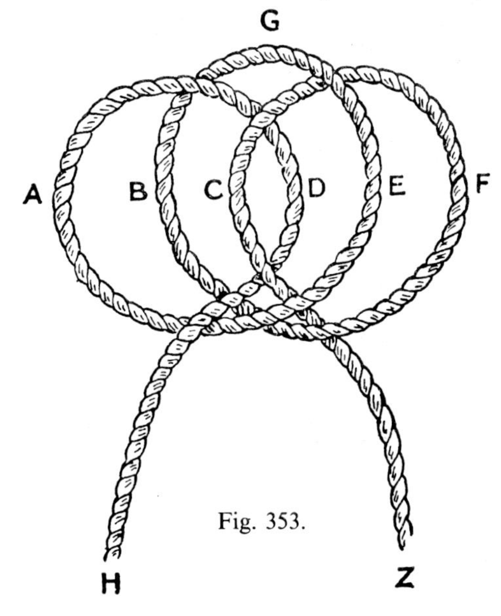

Fig. 353.

It is formed by three half-hitches. Two of these are made and laid one behind the other, *A* and *B* (Fig. 353). A third hitch, *C*, is then made and slipped in behind hitch *B* and over hitch *A* all as shewn in Fig. 353. This completes the first stage.

Now take *C* and draw it out under *B* and over *A*, and take *D* and draw it out over *E* and under *F*, and draw out *G*. The ends *H* and *Z* may be either knotted or spliced. Fig. 354 shows the knot completed.

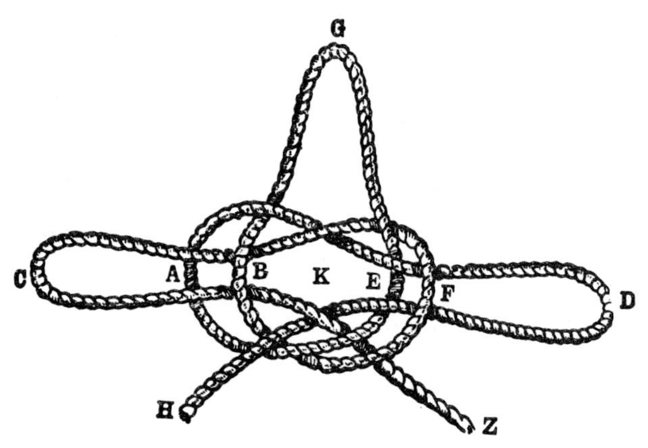

Fig. 354.

A Sling for Round Shot.—This was used for hoisting round shot. It is an adaption of the Jury Knot.

The Jury Knot is made and adjusted so that the three loops and the two ends will enclose the shot.

The loops were seized with spunyarn and the two ends hitched together, leaving a tail *A*, all as shewn in Figure 355.

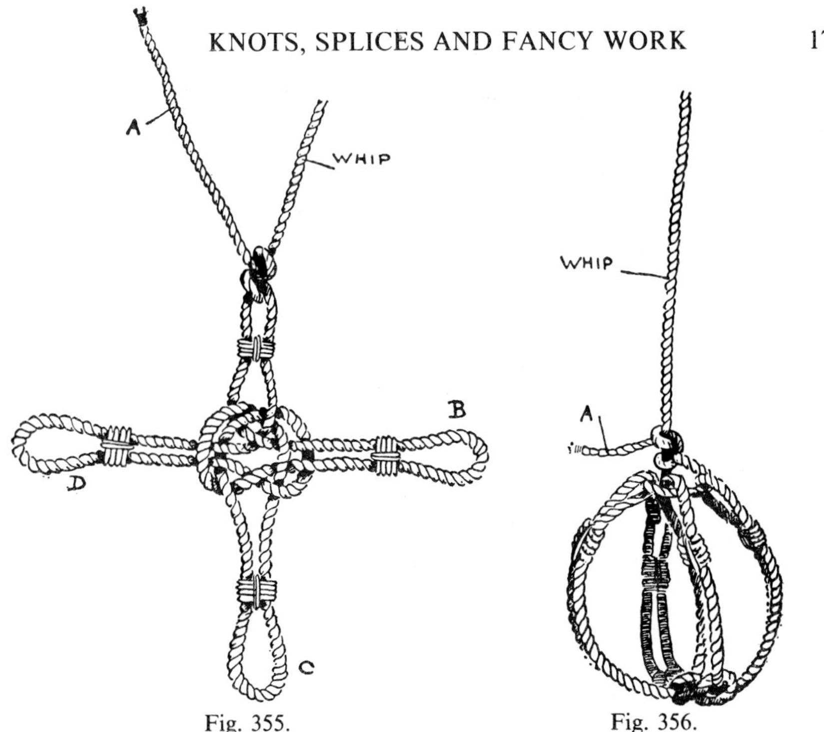

Fig. 355.

Fig. 356.

The shot having been rolled on to the centre of the knot, the short end, or tail *A*, was passed through the three loops *B, C* and *D* and hitched to the whip or hoisting end (Fig. 356).

The shot could be got into or out of the sling by slacking the tail hitches without unreeving the tail from the three loops.

Sling for a Barrel.—The following method of slinging a barrel is adopted when it is desired to hoist it up end on.

Pass the bight *a* of the rope under the lower end of the barrel and bring the two parts up, and with them form an over hand knot *B*, which is opened out so as to fit over the end of the barrel (Fig. 357).

The bight *A* is placed under the cask, and the overhand knot *B* is slipped over the head, and the two ends are brought up and knotted as in Fig. 358.

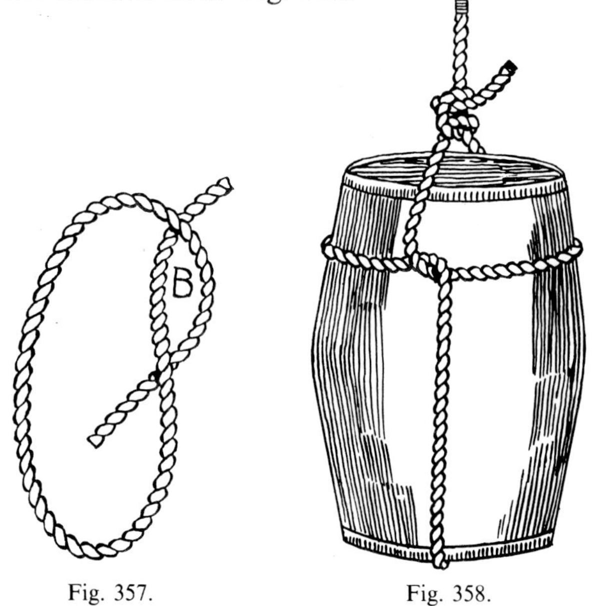

Fig. 357. Fig. 358.

Bag o' Wrinkle.—The most elaborate form of this is made as follows. It is made on a round piece of wood with a groove cut along it. The wood is secured to two stanchions. This form of Bag o' Wrinkle is generally a two-man job but it can be made single-handed. It is a combination of single Coxcombing and Portuguese Sennit. It may of course be used as Coxcombing.

When working two-handed, one man does the Coxcombing (usually with double line) while the other using a separate piece of line does the knotting as in Portuguese Sennit. One man makes a hitch round the stick and the other forms his knot round the bight of the hitch.

When the stick is covered the strands are cut along the groove in the stick (Fig. 359).

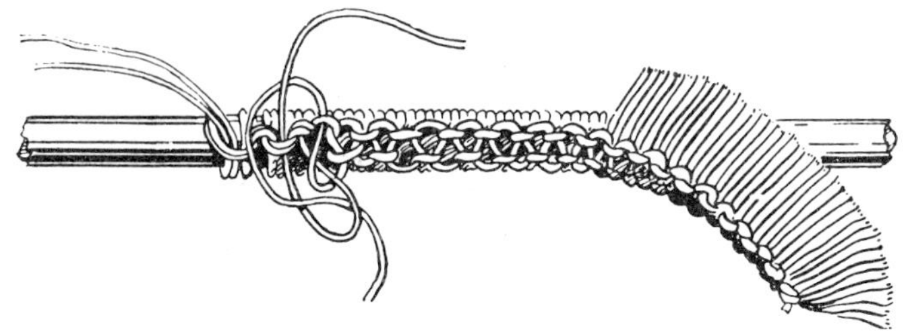

Fig. 359.—Bag o' Wrinkle.

Chafing Gear.—This is made in various ways. It is often called "Bag o' Wrinkle". Thrums are short lengths of stuff.

Bag o' Wrinkle or Railway Sennit.—This was served round stays, topping lifts, backstays, etc. Stretch two pieces of cordage and place the spreader between them. Put the bight of a thrum over the lines and bring the ends of the thrums up between the lines. Haul taut. The sennit is shown in Fig. 360.

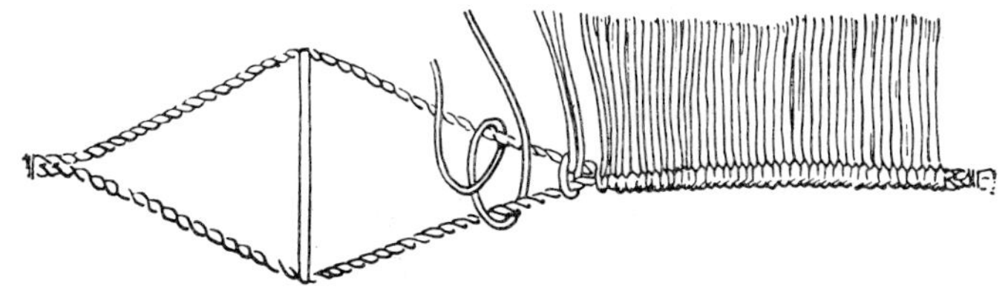

Fig. 360.—Railway Sennit.

Thrum Sennit.—To commence the Sennit take two thrums and middle them round a loop of line, take three of the ends to the right and one to the left. Lay on another thrum alongside the left hand end and over the three right hand ends, as shewn in Fig. 361.

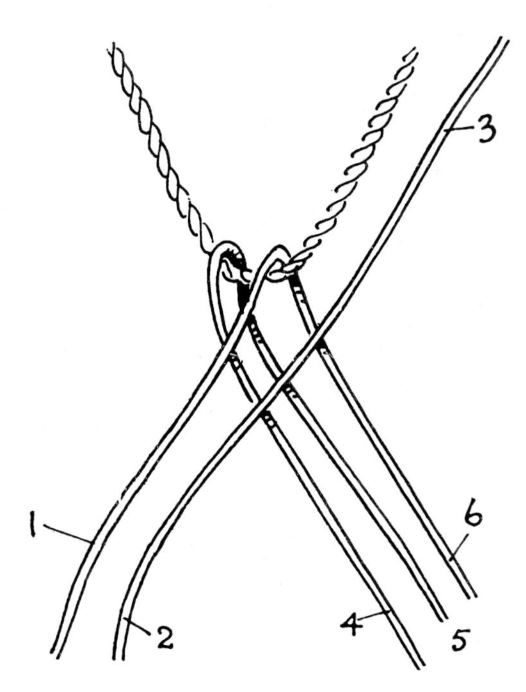

Fig. 361.—Thrum Sennit.

Bring No. 3 end round the back and over ends 1 and 2 laying it parallel to No. 4. Then bring end 6 down over 5, 4 and 3. Numbers 1 and 2 are taken down as part of the fringe.

What was No. 6 now becomes No. 1. Lay on another thrum alongside it and proceed as before (Fig. 362).

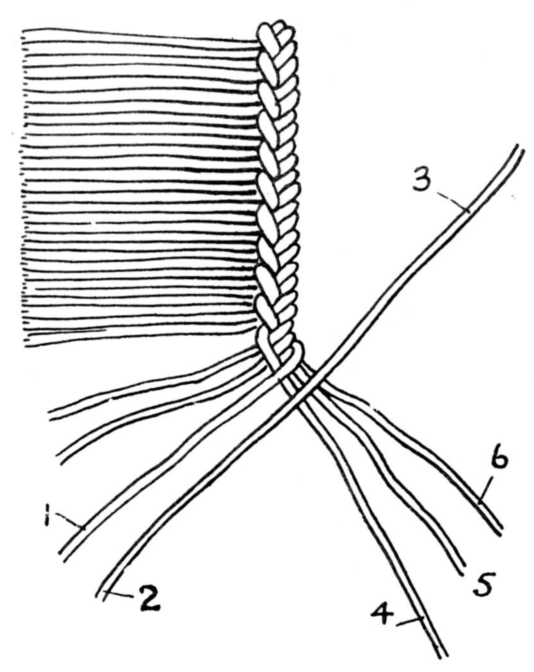

Fig. 362.—Thrum Sennit.

NETTING.

It is not proposed to shew all the processes of making and repairing nets as that has been done in several books on the subject, but an indication of how the work is done follows.

The knot used is the "Single Sheet Bend". The tools used are the netting needle and the mesh gauge, commonly called the mesh. These are shewn in Fig. 363. The string is wound on the needle. The "mesh" is a flat piece of wood or bone of which the width is equal to the length of a one side of a mesh. Very often the "mesh" is not employed, but the second and third fingers of the left hand are used instead.

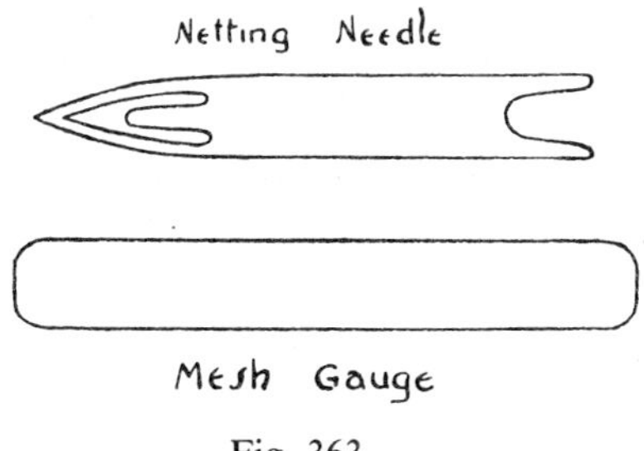

Fig. 363.

Begin by stretching a line as a head rope, then hitch the string to it at equal intervals beginning at the right hand and finishing at the left, so forming the first row, which are half meshes (Fig. 364). The next row is formed by taking the

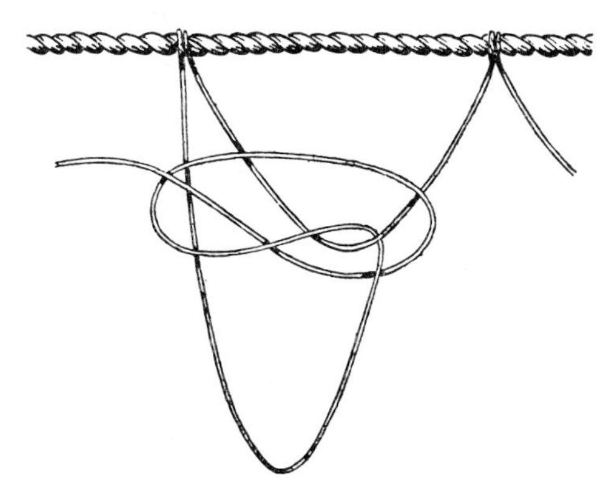

Fig. 364.

string over the "mesh" (not shewn in the figure) up behind it and through the first mesh from back to front. The thumb of the left hand holds the string in place where it passes through the mesh. A loop is then thrown over to the left. Then the netting needle is taken over to the right, behind the first mesh and up through the loop as shewn at *A* (Fig. 364), and the string then pulled tight (Fig. 365, *B*). The process is then

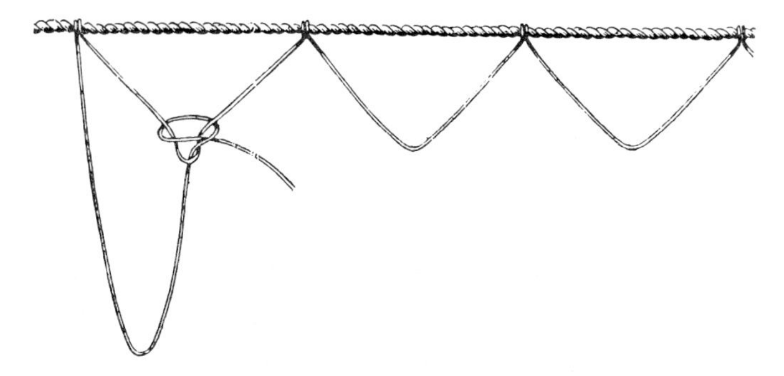

Fig. 365.

repeated on the next mesh always working from left to right. When a row is finished the work is turned over so that work may always be from left to right. In case of a large net it is hung so that the operator can move round to the back.

WORMING, PARCELLING AND SERVING.

Worming consists in laying a strand of marline, spunyarn, etc., in the hollow between the strands of a rope. It should be laid on with the lay. It is used to make the surface of the rope smoother for parcelling and serving. A very thick worming was put on cables near the anchors to protect them against chafe. It was then called keckling (Fig. 366).

Parcelling consists of a bandage of canvas wrapped round a rope. It should be well tarred and laid with the lay of the rope. It is commenced from the bottom and worked upwards so that the overlapping layers tend to shed the water running down the rope (Fig. 366).

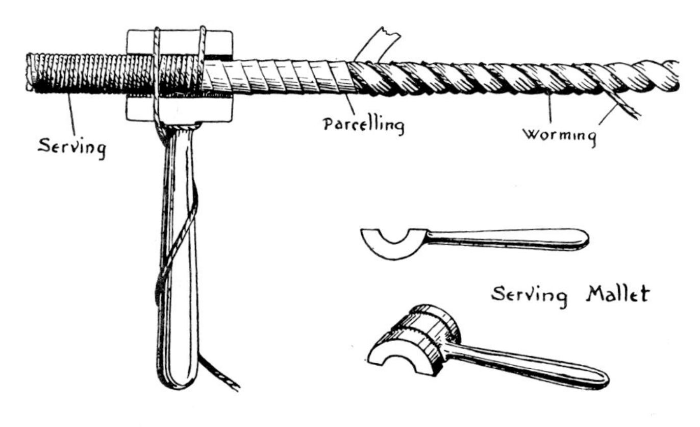

Fig. 366.

Serving is a tight, close binding of marline or spunyarn over wormed and parcelled rope or over a splice, etc. It can be put on "by hand" but where possible ought to be put on with a serving mallet. Fig. 366 shews the mallet in use. It is finished off as in whipping. It is put on against the lay.

GASKETS.

This is how they were made in Nelson's time according to Darcy Lever:

Gaskets are made by taking three or four foxes according to the size, middling them over a pump-bolt, etc.,

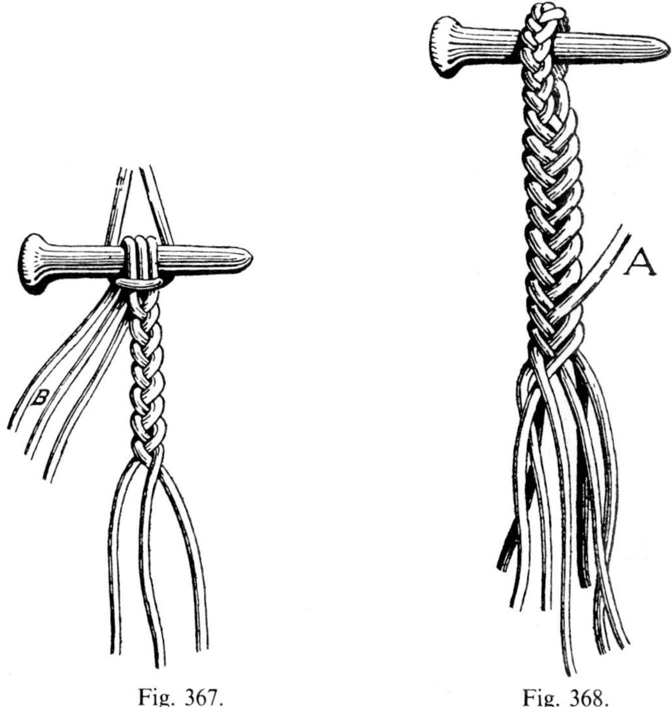

Fig. 367. Fig. 368.

and plaiting the three or four parts together for the length of the eye (Fig. 367). The plaiting is formed by bringing the outside fox on each side alternately over to the middle. The outside one is laid with the right hand and the remainder held and steadied with the left. When this is done, take the other parts, *B* (having shifted the eye part so that it lies over the bolt, Fig. 368) and work the whole together in the same manner; add another fox at *A* and work it for a convenient length, then diminish it towards the end, taking out a fox at intervals. When finished, one end must be laid up, the others plaited, and then the one hauled through.

Chest Lashing.—This is the proper seamanlike way of putting a lashing on a sea chest. The eye *A* is placed on the lid

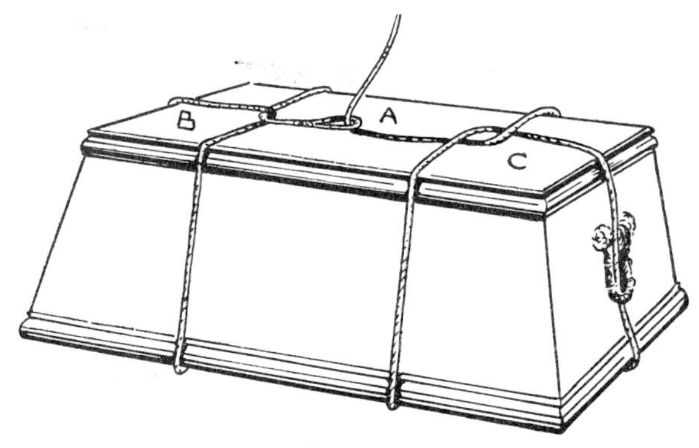

Fig. 369.

of the chest shewn. The lashing is then taken down the back of the chest, under the corner at the bottom and up the end, through the shackle, and over the top to *B* where it is passed round the standing end with the eye. It is then taken down the front of the chest, under the bottom, and passed through the part that was taken across the corner. It is then taken to the right and brought up the front of the chest to *C*. It is then taken down the right-hand end, through the shackle, under the bottom of the chest, through the part that was taken across the corner, and up the back of the chest. It is then passed under at *C* and hitched to the eye.

By putting on the lashing in this way the chest may be opened without taking off the lashing. By combing up the end and throwing the bights over the corner the chest lid may be opened and the weight of the chest keeps the underneath bights in place (Fig. 369).

Scaffold Hitch.—This is used for slinging a plank or staging horizontally. Two round turns are taken over the end of the plank (Fig. 370A). Part 1 is lifted over Part 2 (Fig. 370B). Sufficient of part 2 is then pulled over 1 and 3 and looped over the end of the plank (Fig. 370C). The ends of the rope are pulled to adjust the loops at each side of the plank, then the free end joined into the standing part a few feet above the plank with a bowline (Fig. 370D).

Roadmender's Knot.—This is a hitch used for making a temporary fence by passing a rope from post to post. It can also be used for fastening the end of a rope to a bollard, as it is easily freed after being under strain. Gather up a part of the rope into a long bight (Fig. 371A). Take this around the post below the standing parts (Fig. 371B) and loop it over the top of the post (Fig. 371C).

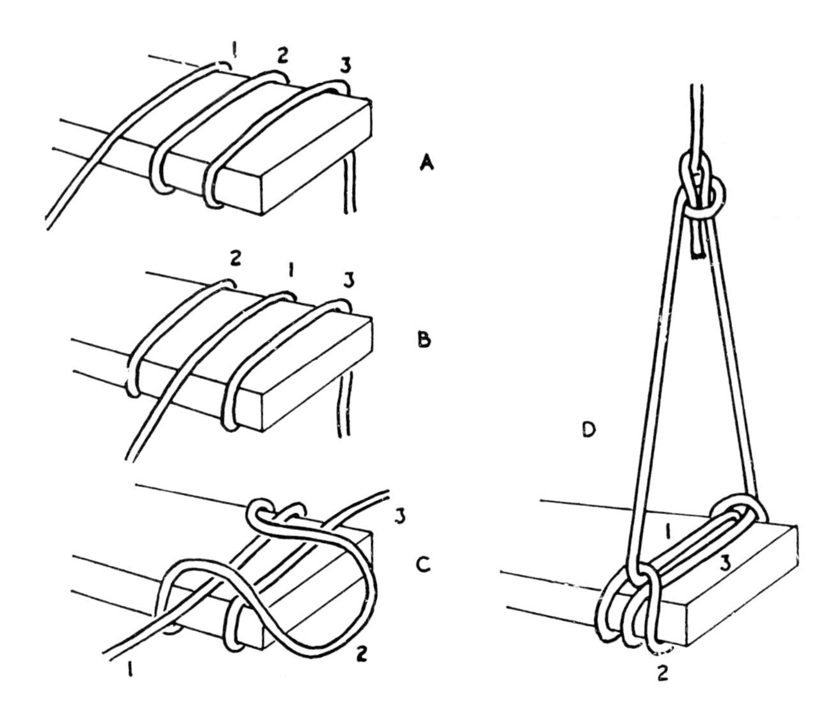

Fig. 370.

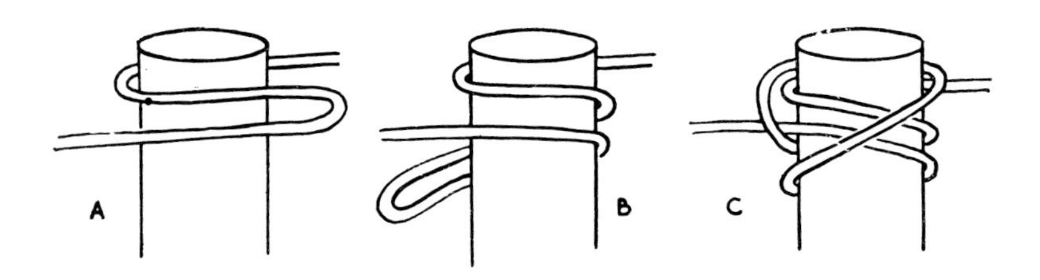

Fig. 371.

Crabber's Knot.—This is a method of forming a running noose, which can be adjusted for size, then converted to a fixed loop. Make a loop and take the end around the standing part (Fig. 372A). Continue under the standing part and form a marine spike hitch (Fig. 372B). When the loop has been adjusted for size, pull parts *X* and *Y* in opposite directions, to make the knot assume a form rather like a bowline on its side (Fig. 372C). This is not as secure as a normal bowline, but it can be trusted to withstand a moderate strain.

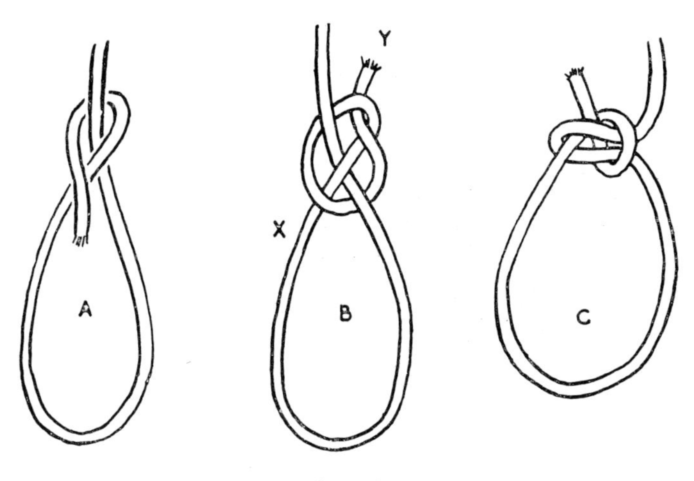

Fig. 372.

Rope Ladder Knot.—This is a method of making a rope ladder without wooden rungs. It is comfortable for use as a bathing ladder, and is easily stowed (Fig. 373). Middle the rope and seize an eye in it. At suitable distances make the knot shown. Bend one rope to an S shape and work the other around it. At the end of the "rungs" the end goes through the loop, but is wrapped intermediately to make up a suitable length. Work alternate rungs in opposite directions to reduce any risk of the ladder twisting.

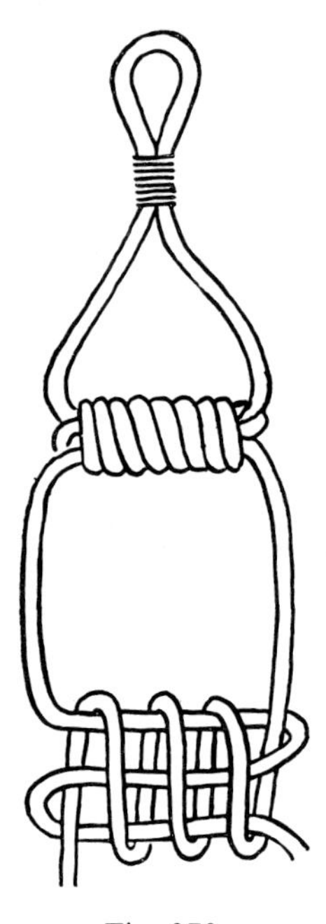

Fig. 373.

SOME NOTES ON SPLICING WIRE ROPES.

It is not proposed to write a complete treatise on splicing wire ropes but only to give sufficient information to enable a handy man to make good and sound splices. There are many other ways equally sound.

For ship work wire ropes maybe said to be always formed of galvanised steel wires.

The rope is almost always six strand laid right handed. It has a hemp heart and in the case of flexible ropes each strand has a hemp heart.

Stiff or hard wire rope, used for standing rigging, is generally made of mild steel wires. For general purposes the wires are made of various kinds of steel, from mild steel to hard drawn plough steel.

The degree of flexibility of wire rope depends on the number and on the size of the wires in each strand. The finer the gauge of the wire the greater the flexibility.

A new kind of wire rope has recently appeared. It is called "Tru-Lay". In this rope each individual wire and each strand is shaped, before being laid up, into the exact spiral form which it will take in the finished rope. One consequence of this is that a strand on being cut, or when it is unlaid from the rope, does not open out or unlay itself. Consequently when working such rope it is not so necessary to whip the ends of strands, so that it is easier to manipulate than ordinary wire rope. It is claimed for this rope also that it gives increased service. In the following notes very special splicing tools are shewn, but for ordinary work on rope up to, say, ¾ in., good marline-spikes will do and a vice is a great convenience.

HOW TO HANDLE WIRE ROPE ETC.

The following article by a wire rope specialist will be read with interest:—

When uncoiling wire rope it is important that no kinks are allowed to form as once a kink is made no amount of

Fig. 374.

strain can take it out, and the rope is unsafe to work. If possible a turn-table should be employed (an old cart wheel mounted on a spindle makes an excellent one); the rope will then lead off perfectly straight without kinks. (See Fig. 374).

If a turn-table is not available the rope may be rolled along the ground as shown in Fig. 375.

Fig. 375.

In no case must the rope be laid on the ground and the end taken over (as in Fig. 376), or kinks will result, and the rope will be completely spoiled.

The life of wire rope depends principally upon the diameter of drums, sheaves, and pulleys; and too much importance cannot be given to the size of the latter. Whenever possible the size of the pulleys should not be less than 700 times the diameter of the largest wire in the rope, and never less than 300 times. The diameters of drums, sheaves and pulleys should increase with the working load when the factor of safety is less than 5 to 1.

The load should not be lifted with a jerk, as the strain may equal three or four times the proper load, and a sound rope may easily be broken.

Fig. 376.

Examine ropes frequently. A new rope is cheaper than the risk of killing or maiming employees.

One-fifth of the ultimate strength of the rope should be considered a fair working load.

In shafts and elevators where human life is constantly raised and lowered, the working load should not be more than one-tenth of the ultimate breaking strength of the rope.

To increase the amount of work done, it is better to increase the working load than the speed of the rope. Experience has shown that the wear of the rope increases with the speed.

Wire rope should be greased when running or idle. Rust destroys as effectively as hard work.

Great care should be taken that the grooves of drums and sheaves are perfectly smooth, ample in diameter, and conform to the surface of the rope. They should also be in perfect line with the rope, so that the latter may not chafe on the sides of the grooves.

Set of Wire Rope Splicing Tools.

To produce the best work, the splicer should have at his disposal a set of tools similar to those in the accompanying illustration (Fig. 377).

The tool set consists of—1 tucker for small strands splicing; 1 marline-spike, round; 1 marline-spike, flatted; 1 pair special steel wire cutters; 1 serving mallet. All of best cast steel, hand forged.

These sets may be had at various prices.

Directions for Splicing.

TO MAKE AN ENDLESS OR LONG SPLICE.—Clamps are applied to the rope sufficiently far back from the ends to allow plenty of room for the splice, and the men to operate in. The two ends are then drawn together by means of blocks and tackle,

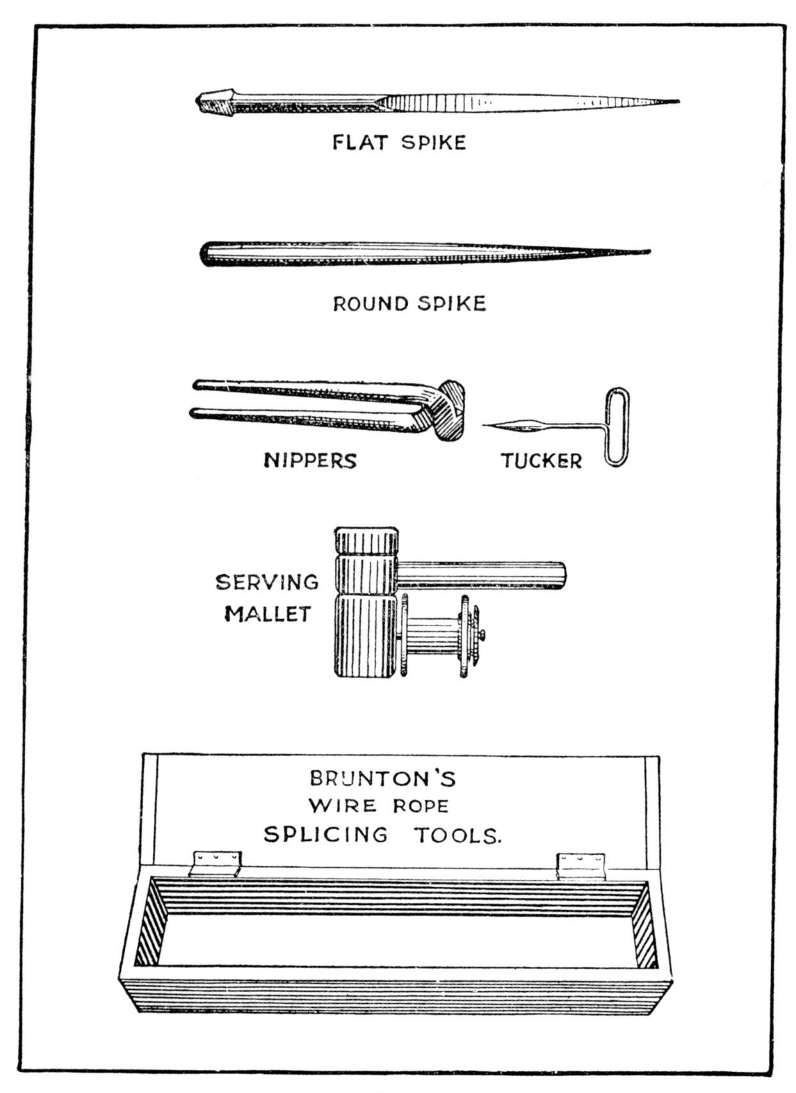
FLAT SPIKE
ROUND SPIKE
NIPPERS
TUCKER
SERVING
MALLET
BRUNTON'S
WIRE ROPE
SPLICING TOOLS.

Fig. 377.

until they overlap each other for a space of 20 to 30 feet, according to the size of the rope. At a point from each end midway of the lap, the rope must be bound with a good serving of No. 18 or No. 20 annealed wire. The serving at the extreme ends is then cut off, the strands untwisted to the new serving, and the hemp cores also cut off so as to abut when the open bunches of strands are brought together, and the opposite strands interlaced regularly with each other, presenting the appearance as near as can be shown (Fig. 378).

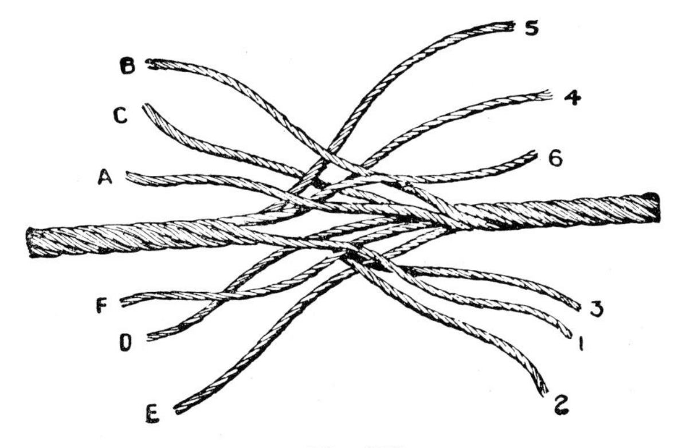

Fig. 378.

After these are all correctly interlaced, pull the ropes tightly together, so that the cores abut against one another. Next take strand No. 1, and as it is being unlaid follow it up with strand *A*, which must be laid into its place tightly until within 5 feet from the end. Strand No. 1 is then cut off, leaving it 5 feet long, same length as *A* strand. The remaining strands are treated the same way, three alternate strands being laid towards the right hand and three to the left. The strands being now all laid in their places, the ends are cut off, as with the first strands, to 5 feet. The appearance of splice will now be the same as in Fig. 379.

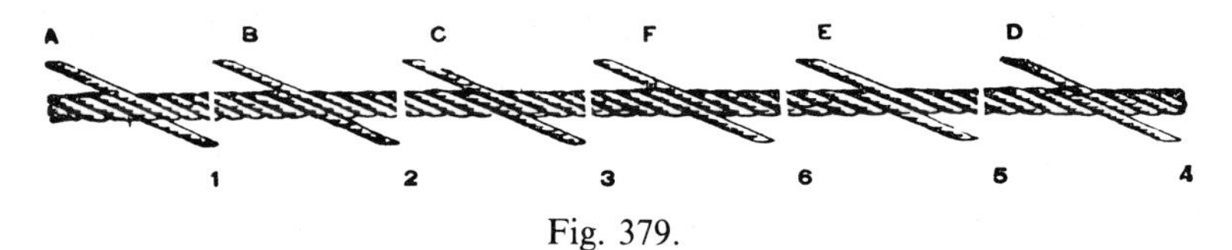

Fig. 379.

The next thing is to tuck in the ends and this is where the skill comes in. *Before doing this, care should be observed to see that the spliced portion of the rope is perfectly limp, or free of tension, otherwise this operation cannot be well performed.* The core is then cut and pulled out on the side corresponding with the end to be tucked in for a distance equal to the length of the end which is to replace it. It is desirable, especially if the rope is composed of small wires, to tie the ends of the strands with soft twine or threads of jute yarn in order to keep the wires well bunched. A marline-spike is then passed over 1 and under two of the strands, when the core is cut off at the proper point, and by moving the spike along the rope spirally with the strands, the loose end 1 is passed into the core space and the spike withdrawn. Then pull out the core on the other side, pass the marline-spike over *A* and under two strands as before, cut off the core, and tuck in the end *A* in precisely the same manner, after which the rope is twisted back again as tightly as possible, and the clamps or other appliances that may be used are removed to the next pair of projecting ends. Any slight inequality in the symmetrical shape of the rope may be taken out by pounding with a wooden mallet. Some prefer to tuck in first all the ends projecting in one direction, and then the ends projecting the other way; it is immaterial in what order they are tucked in. If these directions are implicitly followed, the spliced portion of the rope will be of uniform diameter with other portions and will present a smooth and even appearance throughout. After running a day or two, the locality of the splice cannot be readily detected, and the rope will be quite as strong in this portion as any other.

Splicing Thimbles.

UNDER AND OVER STYLE.—Ordinary type of wire rope. Serve the rope with wire or tarred yarn to suit the circumference of the thimble, bend round the thimble and tie securely in place with temporary lashing till splice is finished (as in Fig. 380). Open out the strands (as in Fig. 381), taking care to keep the loose end of the rope to the left hand. Now insert marline-spike, lifting two strands (as shown in Fig, 382), and tuck away towards the right hand (that is inserting the strand at the point, and over the spike) strand No. 1, pulling the strand well home. Next insert marline-spike through next strand to the left, only lifting one strand, the point of the spike coming out at the same place as before. Tuck away strand No. 2 as before.

Fig. 380.

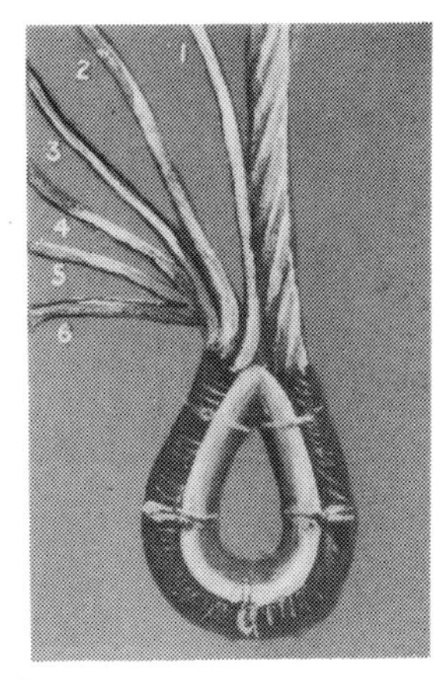

Fig. 381.

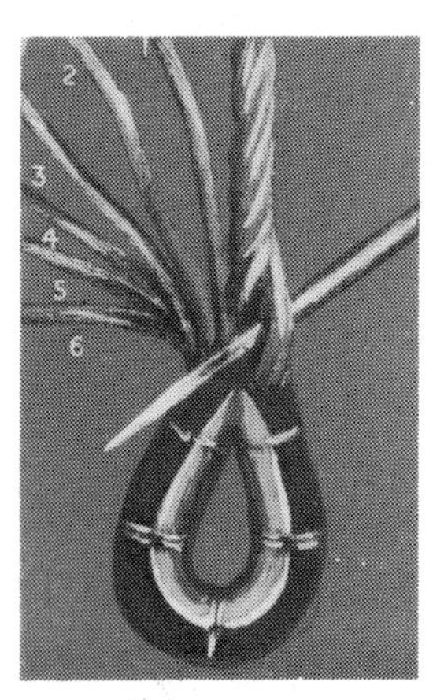

Fig. 382.

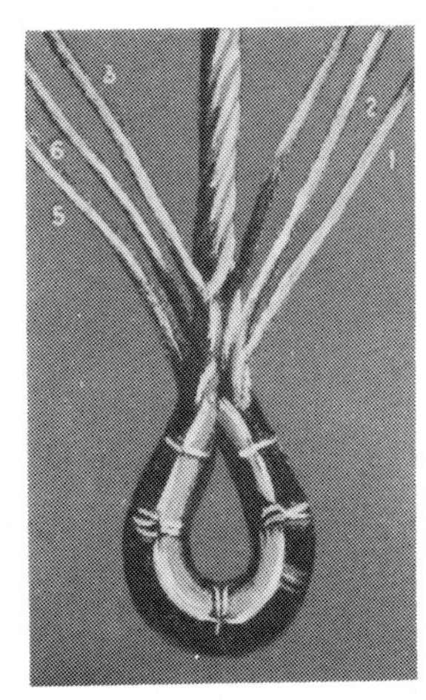

Fig. 383.

The next tuck is the locking tuck. Insert marline-spike in next strand, and, missing No. 3, tuck away strand No. 4 from the point of the spike towards the right hand. Now, without taking out the spike, tuck away strand No. 3 behind the spike towards the left hand (as shewn in Fig. 383). Now insert spike in next strand, and tuck away strand No. 5 behind and over the spike. No. 6 likewise. Pull all the loose strands well down.

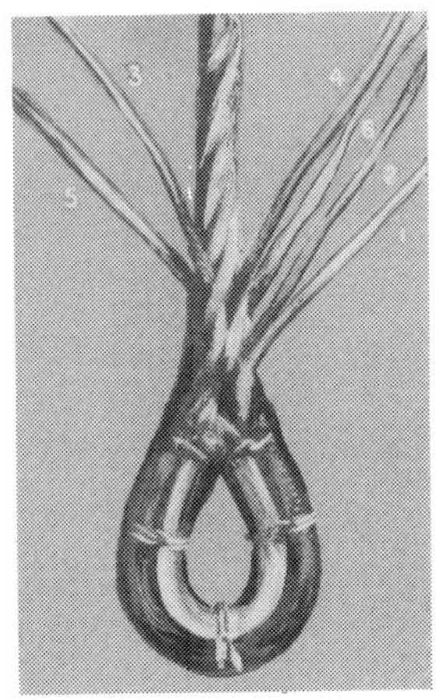

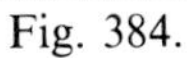
Fig. 384.

Fig. 385.

This completes the first series of tucks, and the splice will, if made properly, be as Fig. 384. Now, starting with strand No. 1, and taking each strand in rotation, tuck away under one strand and over the next strand until all the strands have been tucked four times. If it is intended to taper the splice, the strands may at this point be split, and half the wires being tucked away as before, the other half cut close to the splice. Fig. 385 shows the finished splice ready for serving over.

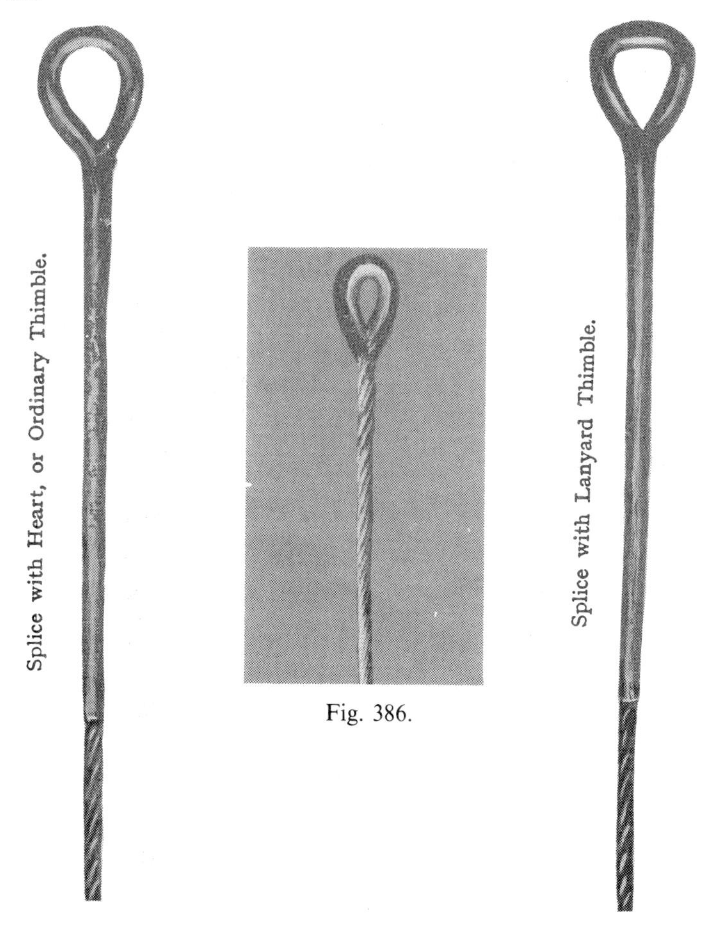

Fig. 386.

It will be noticed that this style of splice possesses a plaited appearance, and the more strain applied to the rope the tighter the splice will grip, and there is no fear of the splice drawing owing to rotation of the rope.

Another, and very good, way is always to tuck "over one strand and under two strands".

LIVERPOOL OR SPIRAL STYLE (see Fig. 386).—Hawsers, or any ropes not hanging free and liable to spin, may be spliced in this style, in which the strands, instead of being interlocked together, are merely tucked round and round one particular strand in the rope. Each loose strand is of course tucked round a different strand in the rope. This is sometimes called the "Liverpool" style.

The figures illustrating the Wire Rope Section have kindly been lent by Messrs. Bruntons (Musselburgh) Ltd., Musselburgh, Scotland.

Wire Grommets.

From Captain Stopford's *Cordage and Cables.*

Take a length of wire rope two and a half times the circumference of the grommet required. Middle it and mark the centre with a whipping. Carefully unlay the strands at one end, stop three together along with the heart, the other three without, being careful not to lose the lay. Unlay these two halves from one another as far as the centre whipping. Then stop the heart in where it lies, cut it and stop the end to the other three strands. Cut off the centre whipping and unlay the remainder, putting a stop round each half before separating them. Each of the halfs will make one grommet.

Then taking one half, turn it to the size of grommet required and mark where the end of the heart (in the middle) comes opposite the heart in the other end. Put on a whipping at this spot and cut off the end of the heart. (The best way to secure the heart is to open out the strands and whip it to the centre one).

Now lay the two ends into the space in the bight, working both ways so as to cover up the ends of the heart and taking care that the heart lies in the place it came from—which can generally be seen. When the two ends meet, marry them and finish off with a long splice. Before tucking, half each strand and take out the heart: tuck one half under one strand and one under two, then each under one. Separate the wires and twist each one until it breaks off, which it will do close down—much closer than you could cut it.

The Perfect Wire Rope Grommet.—It was generally believed that a Wire Rope Grommet of six strands could not be made by laying up a single strand and various methods of getting over the difficulty have been used.

In the books, *Wire Rope Splicing* and *Cordage and Cables*, two of these methods are shewn. It was only after *Knots, Splices and Fancy Work* had been published that the perfect method came to my notice. Like most great discoveries it is very simple but it took a genius to evolve it. The inventor is Archie MacMillan, who is the rigger at Messrs. Wm. Fyfe & Son's yard at Fairlie. His Wire

Grommet is a masterpiece. He has allowed me to publish the method.

Take a length of flexible wire (or strand of a wire rope) of a diameter one-third the diameter of the rope of the desired grommet and about eight times the length of the circumference of the grommet itself.

Begin the grommet in the same way as with hemp rope and follow round till the grommet is of three parts or strands. Then, using a pricker, follow round again, making four parts, then follow round again, using the pricker, and lightly beating with a hammer at every turn so as to lay the fifth strand well in.

Now comes the touch of genius. Take a piece of the same wire rope of such a length that it will lie right round the grommet with an inch or two to spare. With the pricker work this piece in as a heart in the centre of the five strands already laid, leaving the two ends sticking out. It will be found that another strand can now be laid in with the pricker, thus making six strands.

The ends are now tucked right through the centre of the grommet, that is with three strands above and three strands below them. The temporary heart is now pulled out and the two ends are laid in its place. Each end is taken round the grommet half-way and the two are cut off so that they just meet. They thus form the heart of the grommet.

APPROXIMATE STRENGTH OF ROPE

Hemp.	Iron.	Steel	Working Load. Cwts.	Breaking Strain. Tons.	Ordinary Chain. (diameter)
(circumference)					
2¾	1		6	2	5/16
	1½	1	9	3	
3¾	1⅝		12	4	
	1¾	1½	15	5	
4½	1⅞		18	6	
	2	1⅝	21	7	
5½	2⅛	1¾	24	8	9/16
	2¼		27	9	
6	2⅜	1⅞	30	10	
6½	2⅝	2	36	12	
	2¾	2⅛	37	13	
7	2⅞	2¼	42	14	11/16
7½	3⅛	2⅜	48	16	
8	3⅜	2½	54	18	
	3½	2⅝	60	20	
8½	3⅝	2¾	66	22	
9½	3⅞	3¼	78	26	15/16
10	4		84	28	1
	4¼	3⅜	90	30	
11	4⅜		96	32	
	4½	3½	108	36	
12	4⅝	3¾	120	40	

TABLE

Showing Approximate Weights, etc., of Various Cordage.

Kinds.	Length.	Weight.
Reefing twine	24 skeins	8 to 9 lbs.
Sewing twine	24 skeins	8 to 9 lbs.
Marline	12 skeins	4 lbs.
Log lines	25 fathoms	1 to 3 lbs.
Samson lines	30 fathoms	¾ lb.
Samson lines	30 fathoms	1 lb.
Samson lines	30 fathoms	1¼ lbs.
Samson lines	30 fathoms	1½ lbs.
Fishing lines	25 fathoms	¼ lb.
Fishing lines	25 fathoms	½ lb.
Fishing lines	25 fathoms	¾ lb.
Fishing lines	25 fathoms	1 lb.
Hambro'-lines (6 threads)	23 fathoms	1½ lbs.
Hambro'-lines (9 threads)	23 fathoms	2¼ lbs.
Hambro'-lines (12 threads)	23 fathoms	3 lbs.
Hand lead lines	120 fathoms	4 lbs.
Deep sea lines	120 fathoms	28 lbs.
Deep sea lines	120 fathoms,	32 lbs.
Deep sea lines	120 fathoms	34 lbs.
Deep sea lines	120 fathoms	36 lbs.

Approximate Strength of Short Round-Linked Chain.

Inches.	Mean Breaking Strain. Tons.	Test.
1¼	44	18·8
1	29	12·0
⅞	23	9·1
¾	17	6·8
⅝	12	4·6
½	7½	3·0

TABLE OF WEIGHTS AND APPROXIMATE BREAKING STRAINS

Circumference of Rope	White & Lightly Tarred Italian Hemp	White Manila Rope		Tarred Hemp Rope		Coir Rope		Galvanised Rigging Wire Rope		Galvanised Patent Steel Flexible Wire Rope		Galvanised Patent Steel Extra Flexible Wire Rope		Circumference of Rope
	Breaking Strains	Weight for 120 Fathoms	Breaking Strain	Weight for 120 Fathoms	Breaking Strain	Weight for 120 Fathoms	Breaking Strain	Weight per Fathom	Break-ing Strain	Weight per Fathom	Break-ing Strain	Weight per Fathom	Break-ing Strain	
Ins.	Cwts.	Ct. Qr. Lb.	Tns. Cwts.	Ct. Qr. Lb.	Tns. Cwts.	Ct. Qr. Lb.	Tns. Cwts.	Lbs.	Tons.	Lbs.	Tons.	Lbs.	Tons.	Ins.
1	—	—	—	—	—	—	—	1·2	1¾	·76	1¾	·88	2½	1
1¼	—	—	—	—	—	—	—	1·6	3	1·12	2⅞	1·36	4	1¼
1½	27	—	—	—	—	—	—	2·2	4	1·44	4	2·00	7	1½
1¾	37	—	—	—	—	—	—	3·0	5½	2·00	5½	2·72	9	1¾
2	50	0 3 4	1 6	1 0 0	0 19	0 2 4	0 6	3·8	7	2·40	7	3·48	11	2
2¼	65	0 3 26	1 13	1 0 27	1 2	0 2 19	0 8	4·6	9	3·12	9½	4·44	13½	2¼
2½	80	1 0 20	2 0	1 2 4	1 7	0 3 9	0 10	5·8	11	4·00	12½	5·44	17½	2½
2¾	97	1 1 25	2 9	1 3 11	1 13	1 0 0	0 12	6·8	13	4·64	15½	6·72	22½	2¾
3	116	1 3 2	2 18	2 0 22	2 2	1 0 22	0 14	8·0	16	5·48	18	8·00	25½	3
3¼	—	2 0 7	3 8	2 2 10	2 7	1 1 17	0 16	9·2	19	6·80	22	9·48	30	3¼
3½	157	2 1 12	3 19	3 0 2	2 17	1 2 15	0 19	11·2	22	7·80	26	11·00	36	3½
3¾	—	2 2 21	4 11	3 1 21	3 7	1 3 14	1 2	12·4	26	9·00	29	12·44	40	3¾
4	—	3 0 6	5 3	4 0 0	3 17	2 0 16	1 5	14·4	30	10·00	33	14·24	44	4
4¼	—	3 2 0	5 17	4 2 0	4 4	2 1 18	1 8	17·0	34	11·20	35	16·00	49	4¼
4½	—	3 3 20	6 11	4 3 24	4 10	2 2 20	1 12	18·4	38	12·80	39	18·00	50	4½
5	—	4 2 24	8 2	6 0 15	5 10	3 1 8	2 0	—	—	—	—	—	—	5
5½	—	5 3 16	9 16	7 1 15	6 10	4 0 0	2 8	—	—	—	—	—	—	5½
6	—	7 0 8	11 13	8 3 4	8 9	4 3 4	2 18	—	—	—	—	—	—	6
6½	—	8 1 0	13 14	10 1 12	9 9	5 2 12	3 6	—	—	—	—	—	—	6½
7	—	9 1 20	15 18	12 0 8	11 9	6 2 4	3 18	—	—	—	—	—	—	7
8	—	12 0 24	20 14	16 0 0	15 9	8 2 8	5 0	—	—	—	—	—	—	8